AFFAIR
RECOVERY

A 4-Step Process to
Healing, Forgiveness, and Growth

ANDREW McCONAGHIE, LCSW

 **MC Publishing**

Affair Recovery: A 4-Step Process to Healing, Forgiveness, and Growth
Andrew McConaghie, LCSW

Copyright © 2021

All rights reserved. No part of this publication may be reproduced, stored in retrieval system, or transmitted in any way by any means, electronic, mechanical, photocopy, recording or otherwise without the prior permission of the author except as provided by USA copyright law.

ISBN: 978-1-7376233-1-1 (paperback), 978-1-7376233-0-4 (epub)

Publishing and Design Services: MelindaMartin.me

DEDICATION

Thanks to my wife, Tracy,
who has always been my biggest fan
and encouraged me to write this book.

Also, many thanks to
all of the couples over the years
who have allowed me to witness their courage
and strength in the process of healing their
relationships after an affair.

CONTENTS

Introduction 1

Chapter 1 Questions, Questions, Questions 5
Chapter 2 Anatomy of an Affair 13
Chapter 3 Managing the Initial Crisis as a Couple 21
Chapter 4 Managing the Initial Crisis as Individuals 29
Chapter 5 Forgiveness 35
Chapter 6 Steps in the Forgiveness Process 41
Chapter 7 Step 1: What Actually Happened? 49
Chapter 8 Step 2: Empathy for the Betrayed 55
Chapter 9 Step 3: Understanding Why the Affair Occurred .. 77
Chapter 10 Step 4: The Leap of Faith 93
Chapter 11 Factors that Affect Recovery 105
Chapter 12 A Message of Hope 111

Appendix: Truths and Tips to Hold On To 113

About the Author 124

Introduction

This book is for couples who are experiencing or have experienced a significant betrayal such as an affair, yet still have hope that they can find a way to heal and stay together. Although you may be in the depths of despair now, somewhere in those emotions you may also find feelings of commitment and love. You can heal your relationship if you and your partner are willing to participate in the forgiveness process outlined in these chapters. The 4-Step Affair Recovery Process that I have developed over the many years I've worked with couples often has produced profound results. Many couples manage not only to heal from the affair, but also to acquire the skills and characteristics that will move them forward in their relationships to new points of growth. These skills include meaningful communication, problem solving, connection, and ongoing forgiveness. The fact of the matter is that all long-term relationships require repair and forgiveness on some level in order to maintain love and intimacy for the long haul. Without forgiveness, a relationship is weakened as resentment builds and a couple's connection erodes, putting the relationship at risk.

Repairing a relationship after an affair will take tremendous work. You will both need to be committed to each other in order to find the patience required to manage your emotional responses during this slow and difficult process. You will both also need to put yourselves in emotionally challenging and vulnerable places you may never have been with each other.

Even with this level of commitment, there is no guarantee that you will stay together. However, if you as a couple go through this process successfully, it can be transformative for your relationship as well as for each of you as an individual. Even if the relationship ends, the benefits you will receive will follow you into any future relationships you might have, whether romantic or otherwise.

If you are a couples counselor or therapist and want to guide couples on this path of healing and improving their relationships, this book can also be a useful tool for you. My hope is that you will find practical ideas here as you take this difficult yet satisfying journey with your clients.

Finally, a word about who this book is *not* for. My forgiveness process will not work if the person who committed infidelity is not willing to end contact with the other person in the affair. It also will not be useful for a person who wishes to get revenge on their partner or level the playing field by, for example, having their own affair. In addition, to successfully utilize the strategies in this book, both members of the relationship must be willing to be completely honest. Holding back the truth out of fear of the consequences, even with the intention of protecting your partner or yourself, will sabotage your progress. Finally, this book will not help you get your partner to stay with you. There are no tricks or tools to compel an unwilling partner to remain in a relationship. If they do not wish to be in the relationship, the best you can do is focus on your own individual healing and know that you deserve and can obtain happiness and respect once again.

In most cases, I use the term "partner" to describe an individual in a relationship because it is the most inclusive choice. Affairs

Introduction

happen among people who are married, engaged, and dating, and to both homosexual and heterosexual couples. The case studies in this book represent heterosexual couples simply because most of my work experience has been with this population. However, I hope this book will feel accessible to all.

Also, I have decided to mostly use the word "affair," recognizing that people have various interpretations of this word. For simplification, I am defining an "affair" (or "cheating" or "betrayal") as a situation in which someone has an improper relationship with another person outside of his or her primary relationship. Such a relationship usually involves secrecy, indicating that on some level, the person is aware that they are betraying their partner. Affairs can take various forms, from a sexual relationship to a physical, non-sexual relationship to one that is purely emotional in nature. It can be an in-person relationship or one developed and maintained through technology. Whatever term you and your partner decide to use to describe the other relationship, consistency is important, with each other and with your therapist.

I use many stories to illustrate concepts or experiences throughout this book. In every case, names and circumstances have been changed to protect privacy. In fact, each illustration is actually a composite of couples I have worked with and does not specifically represent any one situation I have encountered. Any similarities to actual couples are purely coincidental.

I'd also like to mention the challenging role that shame can play in the aftermath of an affair. In my training as a therapist, I was fortunate to study under Dr. Brené Brown, the bestselling author and researcher on shame. Here is Dr. Brown's definition of shame and its damaging effects on a person and their relationships:

I define shame as the intensely painful feeling or experience of believing that we are flawed and therefore unworthy of love and belonging—something we've experienced, done, or failed to do makes us unworthy of connection.

I don't believe shame is helpful or productive. In fact, I think shame is much more likely to be the source of destructive, hurtful behavior than the solution or cure.

Since shame is a powerful emotion that can impede the reconnection of a couple, you will need to be ready to continually address it throughout my 4-Step Affair Recovery Process. To help with this exploration, at the end of Chapters 7–10 I will briefly walk you through the different ways shame can show itself and some ways you can address it.

Finally, at the end of each chapter, I have included key truths about recovering from an affair that can act as anchors of hope and guide posts throughout your healing process. All of these are also found in the Truths and Tips to Hold On To appendix. My sincere wish is that this book will positively contribute to your understanding as a couple or a counselor of the power of forgiveness and the miracle of reconciliation.

CHAPTER 1

Questions, Questions, Questions

To begin, I will address the most common questions that trouble couples once an affair is discovered. The answers to these questions provide an overview of affairs and follow a person's path through this traumatic experience.

Why did this happen?

From the beginning, you may both struggle with this question. Making sense of infidelity may be difficult because the behavior can seem confusing and out of character for the person who had the affair. The confusion creates a significant amount of anxiety as both partners try to make sense of what has happened. In order to help lower that anxiety, we need to address this question directly.

I have found that affairs are caused by multiple factors that develop over time. In many cases, an underlying sense of profound unhappiness in one or both partners plays a large part. This unhappiness can be related to emotional distance or conflict in the primary relationship, or it can have little to do with the relationship and be a part of an individual's personal struggles. In our society, there are common misconceptions about what type of person cheats or has an affair. Often, the cheating partner is viewed as uncaring, sex-crazed, morally degenerate, or even sociopathic for engaging in these behaviors. Many people assume that betrayal is related to a lack of sex in their primary relationship or a loss of attraction to the other partner. In my work with couples, I have not found any of these dynamics to be consistently true. If they are present, they are outliers. My experience is that most partners who have affairs are good, honest people who are struggling the way most of us are. They just happen to engage in these specific unhealthy, destructive behaviors in response to their struggles. This question will be addressed more thoroughly in Chapter 2 and Chapter 9.

Is it possible ever to feel better?

The short answer is "Yes," though it may be hard to believe now because of the hopelessness, sadness and other emotions you are feeling. Addressing this issue now in a straightforward and productive manner will lead to feeling better in the long run. As surprising as it may sound, many couples have reported to me that, although recovering from an affair was one of the most difficult experiences of their lives, it was also an unexpected blessing because it forced them to address issues they had kept buried for years. They are now happier, healthier, and more connected than ever before.

Should I stay or should I go?

The best answer to this question is that it does not need to be decided immediately. In fact, I strongly urge you not to make that decision yet (see Chapter 3). It is empowering to know that ultimately you have a choice whether to stay or leave. Both options have positive and negative consequences. This book and a trained therapist can help you and your partner find clarity about which decision is best for you.

If I choose to stay, will we ever have a good relationship?

I hope that anyone who chooses to stay long term in a relationship will only do so because the relationship is positive and healthy, or at least has the potential to be so. Many couples who can work through the aftermath of an affair in a productive way end up with wonderful relationships. Of course, there are times when this does not happen, often because one or both partners can't or won't do the honest work required. Other times, one individual or the other may simply come to the conclusion that this relationship is not the path they would like to continue to pursue. In any case, my hope is that healing can occur between individuals for their own sakes and for the benefit of their children (if they have any), whether or not they stay together.

Will other people look down on us for either staying together or separating following an affair?

They certainly might. Many people have strong judgments about how couples should handle an affair. Some believe that people should stay in a relationship, especially a marriage, no matter what, at virtually any cost. Others feel that no one should ever stay with someone who cheats on them. It is important to realize that ultimately the people involved in the relationship are the experts about what is healthiest for them. The wide variety of opinions about how to handle infidelity is a good enough reason to be careful about whom you talk to about your relationship. In Chapter 3, I'll guide you through this topic a bit more.

Will I ever trust my partner again (or will my partner ever trust me again)?

Couples often feel a sense of hopelessness about this question, especially early in the process. Doubt about whether you can trust again may even affect your willingness to participate in the forgiveness process, since, without the possibility to trust again, trying to repair your relationship seems like a waste of time. While this concern is valid, readers should take comfort in the fact that I have time and time again seen couples regain trust following an affair. Of course, the potential for trust depends upon many factors concerning both partners in the relationship. My 4-Step Affair Recovery Process outlined in chapters 7–10 discusses these factors in detail.

Is it normal for me to have all these crazy emotions?

The emotions you feel are always normal and valid. An affair is an intense and often traumatic experience for each person involved. The process outlined in this book includes exploring these emotions, why you are experiencing them, and what can help you to move forward past them. The best step both of you can take for now is to accept your own feelings and those of your partner without judgment. Doing so will help you as a couple to understand the feelings that often accompany an affair and, ultimately, to move beyond them.

Is it my fault that my partner cheated on me?

No, it is not. A problematic relationship can be vulnerable to affairs, but an affair is the full responsibility of the person who has engaged in it. Often people have affairs for reasons that have little or nothing to do with the relationship. Even if an affair is influenced by a troubled relationship, it is never the fault of the one who was cheated on. Everyone is responsible for their own behavior.

I don't know my partner (who cheated) anymore. Who is he/she?

Finding out about an affair can be incredibly disorienting. This is a normal response. You may feel as though you know exactly how the world and your partner work, only to discover a terrible truth that undermines everything you had believed. Although there are occasions on which a person has been conned by their partner, usually this is not the case. Good people can make some pretty bad mistakes. The mistake of an affair does not necessarily mean that the qualities of the person you fell in love with are nonexistent now.

People who have been cheated on often experience the phenomenon called *cognitive dissonance* for some time. Cognitive dissonance is the state of having inconsistent thoughts or beliefs. When dealing with an affair, it might be very difficult for you to believe that your partner could both cheat on you and still love you, or wants to stay with you, or is still a good person with good character. The improbability of any of these possibilities can leave a person feeling very out of balance and stressed.

Another common internal conflict happens when your decision to stay in the relationship defies your belief that if anyone ever cheated on you, you would leave. Now that you are faced with this reality, you may realize that the decision is not an easy one to make. You may change your mind, choosing to stay and work things out in the relationship.

One of the goals of the 4-Step Affair Recovery Process is to reconcile these seemingly opposing truths in order to understand that both can be true. When this happens, *assimilation,* that is, taking two seemingly opposing truths and reconciling them into one truth, can occur. For example, a good, caring person can also do bad, uncaring things; or a person who loves someone else can, at times, behave in a very unloving way towards that person.

Truths and Tips to Hold On To

- Questions are a normal part of the healing process after an affair.

- It is important to address these questions directly, even if the answers are not immediately forthcoming.

- Until these questions are addressed, you will not have the clarity you need to make decisions about moving forward in your relationship.

- Because people outside of your relationship will have varying opinions, be careful about whom you choose to speak to about the affair.

- You should never blame yourself (or take the blame for) your partner's infidelity.

- Cognitive dissonance, the state of having inconsistent thoughts or beliefs, is a normal response to an affair.

- Assimilation, the reconciliation of seemingly opposing truths, is an important step in the healing process after an affair.

Now that we've covered some of the pressing questions following the discovery of an affair, let's take a look at some of the typical characteristics of an affair.

CHAPTER 2

Anatomy of an Affair

What is an affair? Most people define an affair as sex outside of marriage or any other committed relationship. However, the definition of an affair is actually much broader. An affair or *cheating* can include a flirtatious e-mail or text correspondence, a secret emotional relationship, a full sexual encounter, or simply looking at pornography. Whether or not one's behavior is a betrayal depends upon whether or not one's partner perceives it as such. This perception is based upon the agreements that exist between two people in a relationship. If one of the members of the relationship breaks one of these agreements or promises, the feelings of betrayal and broken trust can indicate an affair.

These agreements can be explicit or implicit. Explicit agreements are the type that partners communicate directly to each other. For example, couples often explicitly agree not to have sex outside of marriage by the act of getting married. They may also say directly to each other that they agree not to use pornography, or they may agree that pornography is acceptable in their relationship. An implicit agreement is one that has not been clearly discussed but that at least one of the partners believes is an expectation in the relationship. For example, a woman might assume that her partner would never frequent a strip club, even though the couple never discussed such behavior directly. Her partner, on the other hand might assume it is fine with her if he goes to a strip club because she has never said otherwise. If one of the parties believes a promise or agreement existed, and that agreement is broken, then the resulting feeling of betrayal requires attention in the relationship.

Certain signs point to a problem behavior or betrayal in cases that are not the obvious sex-outside-of-marriage situation. The primary clue that this might still constitute affair behavior is secrecy, either through lying directly or omitting information. Feelings of guilt or even a feeling of angry entitlement—convincing oneself that the behavior should be allowed—might be present. The bottom line is that if someone intentionally keeps information from a spouse or partner, then, on some level, they know the partner would be uncomfortable or unhappy with the behavior and therefore would perceive it as a betrayal.

Why do people cheat? Many people assume that those who choose to be unfaithful are selfish people with no character. In my experience counseling hundreds of couples who have experienced infidelity, it is much more complicated than that. In fact, there are many reasons individuals make the unfortunate choice to cheat. Throughout this book, I will attempt to balance the reality of personal accountability with a contextual understanding of why people do what they do. Looking at the causes of people's behavior in no way excuses their actions or dismisses those people from having to deal with the consequences. The following three stories illustrate a few, but not all, of the common infidelities that can impact a relationship.

Story #1: Marjorie and Devon

Marjorie is married and has two young children with her husband, Devon, who is their primary caretaker throughout the day. Marjorie has been successful at her job, which requires her to travel frequently. She feels the responsibility of financially taking care of the family, but also feels stressed when she is at home because of the kids and her difficult relationship with Devon. Devon feels overwhelmed by the demands of caring for the children and gets frustrated when Marjorie has to travel, which often leads to arguments. The more they argue, the more time Marjorie spends away from the house. She feels criticized and unappreciated. During this time, a male coworker called Dan starts to show her more and more attention. He is single with no children and seems to appreciate Marjorie's dedication to work, as well as her intelligence.

At first, Marjorie and Dan only spend time together at the office for work, but then they occasionally start going to lunch together to discuss business projects. Marjorie starts to feel a bit guilty, but is able to justify their meetings as necessary to her job. After a few months, Dan gets a promotion and starts to travel to the same conferences that Marjorie attends. As their friendship grows, it gradually becomes flirtatious. Marjorie enjoys the attention and tells herself that there is nothing wrong with flirting back a little. This behavior goes on for a while until they are together at a conference out of town and meet for a drink at the end of the day. That night, they end up having sex. Marjorie feels guilty but is able to justify the relationship in her mind. She tells herself that her husband has no time for her, has not been interested in sex for months, and only finds ways to criticize her. Marjorie also convinces herself that if Devon doesn't know about the other guy, it won't hurt him. After all, she deserves to be happy, and it is not really hurting anyone if he doesn't know.

Story #2: Sherry and Abraham

Sherry always wanted to get married and have children. She has been married to Abraham for ten years and has willingly given up her career to take care of their son. However, Sherry has been increasingly dissatisfied with her life. She doesn't feel successful as a mother due to her son's challenging behavior. She also doesn't feel attractive to her husband, who has become more distant over the years. Sherry misses the time when she was appreciated at work and pursued by Abraham.

Recently, her son's soccer coach Manuel has been spending more time speaking with her at practices. In fact, he gives Sherry his cell phone number to call in case she had any questions about how her son is doing in soccer. This quickly turns into daily phone conversations about her unhappiness in life. Manuel is such a good listener and seems to genuinely understand and care about her. One day, when they are talking on the phone, he suggests meeting for coffee to continue their conversation face to face. Since her son is at school, they start to meet frequently during the day. Sherry finds herself looking forward to their meetings more than anything in her life. Soon, Manuel begins to tell her how wonderful and beautiful she is. Not long after, they begin a physical relationship. Sherry feels terrible about their relationship, but at the same time also becomes obsessed with getting together with him. She loves the way he pursues her and values her intelligence, humor, and beauty.

Story #3: Steve and Jessica

Steve was exposed to sex at an early age when an older child in the neighborhood started showing him pornography. He was just eight years old. By the time Steve was 13, he was looking online at pornographic videos, and started to masturbate on a regular basis. Through high school and college, Steve would masturbate more often, especially at stressful periods *in his life. At 30, Steve is currently in a committed relationship that he hopes will eventually turn into marriage.* He has hidden his daily porn behaviors from his girlfriend Jessica, and hopes that being in a relationship will help him stop fantasizing so much about other women. However, he finds himself continually looking at pornography and eventually starts to reach out to escort services. He loves Jessica and hopes that she never finds out. One day, he hopes to be completely faithful to her and end his other sexual behaviors, but for now he feels trapped by his need for the comfort and stress relief these behaviors provide him. Steve is miserable. He doesn't know why he can't stop doing what he is doing.*

✧

These stories and other incidents of infidelity have some common features. One or both partners are dissatisfied and unhappy with parts of their life. This unhappiness could be caused by problems in the relationship, or by factors that have nothing to do with it. Many people mistakenly assume that their partner will make them happy and when they find themselves in a state of depression or discontent they do not know what to do. In fact, our culture regularly sends unrealistic and mythologized messages about relationships like this. These false messages include the expectation that the initial passion will endure and shouldn't take much effort to keep up. Another misconception is that sex should always feel incredibly new and exciting—and if it is not that way, it must be a sign of a problematic relationship. These types of unfounded beliefs make us particularly vulnerable to the thrill of emotional or sexual attention from someone else.

The other theme present in many incidents of betrayal is the fact that it often gradually grows from an interaction that seems friendly or innocent into something that is much deeper and illicit. Most people do not set out to cheat on their spouse or partner. Rather, they find themselves drawn into a situation that "scratches the itch" of their unhappiness so well that it is difficult to reverse course, even when they feel guilty and unhappy about their choices. I often reference the "boiling frog" metaphor when discussing this process. The metaphor goes like this: When a frog is dropped into boiling water, it immediately jumps out because of the heat. However, if a frog is placed in a pot of water that slowly gets hotter and hotter to the point of boiling, the frog will stay in the water and cook itself. Sometimes a relationship becomes an affair so gradually that the people involved do not recognize the changes until it is too late.

Guilt and shame are also prominent experiences for those who are unfaithful. Most people have an active conscience that on some level makes them feel guilty for their cheating behaviors. I will discuss these dynamics further in the coming chapters, and how shame can interfere with the healing process.

Finally, it is very common for alcohol to play a role in cheating behaviors. The more people drink, the more their better judgment decreases and they lose awareness of their behavior's consequences. People who have put themselves in the position to cheat will be more likely to do so when consuming alcohol. In the moment, they might also use alcohol as an excuse to themselves for their poor choices.

I'd like to mention again at this point that everyone is responsible for their own behavior. Although it is true that complicating factors and an overwhelming sense of unhappiness are often behind infidelity, each person is responsible for what they do with that unhappiness. Many people who are unhappy and discontent do not cheat on their partners, because they use other strategies instead to deal with their stress and pain. For example, people go to therapy, either individually or as a couple, to learn healthy ways of coping with the difficulties of life and relationships. If they are willing to take a hard look at themselves and their living patterns, they can often repair their relationship and can certainly grow into healthier and happier individuals.

Truths and Tips to Hold On To

- ❖ An affair can take many different forms, including flirtatious behavior, a secret emotional connection, a sexual encounter, or looking at pornography.

- ❖ Each couple has implicit and explicit agreements about what constitutes betrayal.

- ❖ Some signs of problem behavior in a relationship include keeping secrets from your partner, outright lying, or omitting information.

- ❖ Our culture teaches that true passion in a relationship lasts forever, a misconception that can lead to feelings of disappointment that cause us to look outside of our relationship for happiness.

- ❖ Feelings of guilt and shame are indicators that your behavior could be perceived as a form of betrayal by your partner.

- ❖ As in the metaphor of the boiling frog, an affair can often creep up gradually, drawing a person in without their full awareness.

- ❖ Alcohol often plays a significant role in poor judgment that leads to an affair.

In the following chapter, I will outline what you can start doing right away as a couple to begin to heal in the weeks immediately following a betrayal.

CHAPTER 3

Managing the Initial Crisis as a Couple

If an affair has just been discovered in your relationship, you are no doubt in a state of crisis. You may feel your world has been turned upside down. You may even feel you are in some kind of a nightmare because this is so unlike how you pictured your life to be. This crisis can be a time of confusion, intense anger (including screaming and shouting), frequent crying spells, and difficulty sleeping or eating. These experiences can apply to both the partner who has been betrayed as well as the partner who has done the betraying. I want to assure you that this difficult period is only temporary and is the natural result of an overwhelming event. The following are strategies for managing this time together as a couple until you get to the next phase, when you are both ready to look at your relationship and the possibility of healing it.

What to Do, What Not to Do

Talking About the Affair

The nature of this crisis can make you want to discuss the affair for hours a day, rehashing details and questions in an attempt to understand it better. On the other hand, you may wish to avoid the topic completely because it feels too painful. Your questions are innumerable; your feelings are immense. Although it is imperative to talk about your questions and feelings, doing so continually can not only be unproductive, but also add to the anxiety and stress you are already feeling, and your emotions can spin out of control.

Still, some time and attention must be given to your experience, so it is also unwise to keep your turmoil hidden inside. I often advise couples to choose a limited portion of each day for these discussions. This should be at a point in the day when work, children, and other distractions won't interfere. Choose a set period of time during the day or early evening, anywhere from 15 minutes to 2 hours, depending upon what suits you as a couple or what your therapist recommends. Outside of those limits, do not discuss the situation. Instead, you may wish to write down your questions or concerns, knowing that you can process them at the agreed-upon time and, of course, in your next therapy session.

Talking about the crisis late at night is often a mistake. I have known couples who start their daily conversation late in the evening and continue into the middle of the night, sleep-deprived and unable to think clearly. During this time, it is very important to take care of your basic needs, including eating, being active, and sleeping. These self-care practices will help you manage this time of extreme stress in a healthier way.

In addition, be careful how you express emotions in these conversations. Emotions will probably be intense when discussing the affair, which is completely understandable and reasonable. However, if these emotions are expressed in a destructive manner, it will bring you further away from your goal of potential healing and reconciliation. Destructive behaviors to avoid include yelling, name-calling, cursing, threatening, getting defensive, and verbally or physically attacking each other. If you and your partner are not able to discuss the affair without these destructive behaviors, it would be best to wait to have the discussion in a therapist's office.

Some couples avoid talking about the affair at all costs. They may want to act as if nothing's wrong because of the pain and difficulty of these conversations. I do not recommend this practice either. Healthy discussions are necessary, even outside of the therapist's office, offering a chance to talk about questions and feelings in the most productive way possible. A therapist can provide structure and teach effective ways to talk about this difficult topic. However, your communication as a couple should not be limited to your weekly therapy appointments.

Additionally, when talking about or processing the affair, be careful to keep children protected. They should not be aware of what happened and how their parents are responding to the affair. Even if you eventually decide to divorce, most of the time children should maintain a healthy relationship with both parents. Knowing about affairs and how the parents are handling them can disrupt and change the relationship between children and their parents for many years in the future. If the children are noticing differences such as how much parents are talking privately or how much emotion the parents are experiencing, it is perfectly fine to mention to them that you are going through a difficult time right now and working through some things as a couple.

Also, be careful not to assume that since the children are asleep, they are safe from hearing these conversations. People get loud when emotional, and children are highly sensitive to trouble between parents. Most are very in tune when something is wrong and they will want to listen, even though doing so is not good for them. It is best to talk in a setting where the children are not present or nearby at all, for example, when they are at school or with a neighbor, grandparents, or a babysitter.

Making Decisions

The immediate aftermath of a revealed or discovered affair is not the right time to make big decisions about your relationship, including whether you should separate or divorce. Remember, this is a time of crisis, which, by definition, means you are over-stressed and unable to think clearly. Separation and divorce are certainly options that you can choose in the future, but to do so during the crisis phase can lead to much greater difficulty later. I recommend that couples agree to take the word *divorce* and any other *exit statements* out of their vocabulary for at least three months while they are working on repairing their relationship. Exit statements are phrases that can indicate that a person potentially is ending the relationship and are generally made in the heat of an argument. They can include comments such as, "I can't keep doing this," "This is never going to work," or "I'm leaving." These statements, even if the person doesn't actually mean them, can be very disruptive and unsettling, especially during the process of repair. If after three months or more, a partner ends up truly considering leaving the relationship either temporarily or permanently, the couple should sit down and talk about this in a productive way, possibly with the help of their therapist.

I also recommend that you proceed cautiously when making decisions such as whether the person who had the affair should move out of the house temporarily or whether or not this person should quit their job if they work with the other person involved in the affair. These decisions are complicated and may have significant consequences to children and others, as well as financial repercussions. I also recommend waiting at least three months to decide on these changes, after consulting your therapist.

Consuming Alcohol

Many couples drink together or are accustomed to drinking in the evenings. I recommend that you avoid alcohol during this time of crisis, especially when you are trying to communicate about your relationship. Avoid discussing the affair when either partner has been drinking even a small amount of alcohol. Most people are not at their best at managing their emotions and using communication skills when they have been drinking, and these talks will need to take place when both individuals are at their best. Consuming alcohol can lead to more impulsivity, more intense emotions, and destructive conversations. Additionally, talking about the affair while drinking usually contributes to feelings of hopelessness and irrational thinking. This is not the time to heighten your emotions further—you want as much clarity as possible to help you make wise decisions and return to a stable emotional place. Avoiding alcohol will also make you more successful at following the other recommendations in this section.

Whom to Tell

Be selective about whom you talk to about the affair. You need support; you need friends and family who will listen. However, some friends and family members in your support circle may put pressure on you to respond the way they think is best. Furthermore, if such people know the details of what happened, they may not be able to manage their own feelings about the unfaithful partner, even if you decide to stay together and move forward in your relationship. I recommend you choose one or two people to rely on for support. Make sure these are people you can trust to keep your confidence, who are able to manage their own emotional responses without adding to your suffering, and who are not likely to be judgmental about what you should or should not do.

Finally, remember that taking care of yourselves is very important during this time. This means sleeping and eating very well, using exercise to relieve stress, and taking breaks from your daily routine to regroup and relax. Some people like to take walks in nature, listen to soothing music, or pay a babysitter so that they can go to a museum or a movie on their own. The goal is for both of you to be as strong and healthy as possible when dealing with this crisis.

Truths and Tips to Hold On To

- Setting aside a certain limited time each day to discuss the affair will give structure to the conversation and also ensure that feelings and questions will get addressed.

- Be careful to keep your children protected from overhearing conversations about the affair.

- Take the word *divorce* and other exit statements out of your vocabulary for at least three months.

- Do not make any major decisions about your relationship, living situation, or job until you are out of this crisis phase.

- Do not talk about the affair late at night or if one or both of you have been drinking.

- Choose only one or two people in your inner circle to talk to about the affair. These people should be trustworthy and able to manage their own emotions about the situation.

- Prioritize self-care at this time to make sure that you are both at your personal best to deal with the intensity of what's happening.

Now let's discuss what each of you can do as individuals to take care of yourself and each other during the initial crisis period following an affair.

CHAPTER 4

Managing the Initial Crisis as Individuals

What to Do, What Not to Do as the Betrayed

Your Questions

You probably have an overwhelming number of questions you want answered as soon as possible. This response is completely understandable, since what has happened was out of your control, and getting as much information as you can might return you to a feeling of stability. You have the right to know any and all information about what happened. However, I suggest that you carefully consider how many details you want to learn about the affair. I have known many people who have demanded and received information that they eventually wished they did not know. For example, explicit details about sexual encounters can cause great distress that may interfere with your peace of mind and ability to forgive your partner in the future. Please understand, you absolutely have the right to this information and may indeed find it helpful in the recovery process. The key will be weighing the benefits and drawbacks of knowing certain facts. A good couples counselor can help you with this difficult assessment.

Investigation

Many men and women who have been betrayed want to investigate as much as possible what happened in the affair. You may have found out about the affair as a result of checking emails, cell phones, and other correspondence. What you initially discovered might prompt you to keep investigating, even after confronting your partner about the affair, because you may believe there is more information that you will never get if you don't look for it yourself. You don't trust your partner because they have kept truths from you and lied to you before. You likely fear they are still hiding things from you.

Some investigating may be helpful so that you can get direct knowledge about some of the details of the affair, but it can also become destructive to you and the relationship. If you are spending hours each day looking for more information, or can't sleep because of all the details swimming inside your head, it is best to pull back from your investigating. If you are neglecting your other responsibilities, such as caring for your children and focusing on your job, you should probably cut back on some of the time you are taking to learn more about the affair. Also, if you continue to feel worse, whether or not you find anything new about the affair, you may be getting obsessed and need to slow down your research efforts. Set some time limits each day regarding how long you will allow yourself to continue to gather more information about the affair. This restriction can help you get to the point of accepting that you have discovered enough information for you to move on with the healing process.

The Wish for Revenge

Watch out for the urge to get revenge. Some people find the need for payback so great that they call their partner's parents or employer to tell them what they have done. Others get in touch with an old boyfriend or girlfriend of their own, or damage property that is precious to the one who has hurt them. Actions like this are impulsive decisions made when you are not at your best. They may feel good in the short term, but will most certainly add to your difficulties in the future, especially if you decide to repair your relationship with your partner. Do your best to manage your emotions and your behaviors, especially during the initial period of finding out about the affair, so that you don't take actions that you eventually will regret.

What to Do, What Not to Do as the Betrayer

The Importance of Honesty

Here's my number-one piece of advice: tell the truth about what happened. You might be thinking that you want to protect your spouse or partner from further hurt, so you shouldn't reveal everything he or she is asking about. You may also feel a tremendous amount of shame and embarrassment, which may keep you from openly disclosing information about your behaviors. Shame causes us to want to keep secrets because of the fear that we are not acceptable to others. However, keeping these secrets will only increase and empower shame. Healing only occurs through openness and vulnerability. I will discuss shame in greater detail in Chapters 7–10 as we go through each of the four steps to forgiveness.

Also, if you want to repair this relationship, the time is now to start rebuilding trust. In the long run, keeping information from your partner will sabotage your chances for success. Your partner's future discovery of what you are lying about or omitting could lead to double the amount of betrayal you both will have to deal with. Furthermore, even if your partner never finds out, you will have to struggle with more secrets you will have to keep forever, along with feelings of guilt and lost integrity. If your relationship is worth saving, it can only be done so with complete honesty. If you want to rebuild trust, proactively telling the whole story will be the best way to start that journey. The more information your partner finds out on their own, the less credible you will be, and the further they will be from trusting you again. Your partner will always wonder if you ever would have told them had they not found out the information themselves. Being truthful and transparent from the beginning of the process will significantly help restore trust within the relationship.

The Need for Patience

Be patient. No doubt your partner is inundating you with questions and demands. They have just discovered what you have been feeling guilty and ashamed about for some time. You may be ready to put an end to the suffering and guilt you have felt since the affair began, but in reality, the process is just beginning for your partner. Listen. Stay as calm as possible. Answer questions without defensiveness or irritation. You may feel inclined to respond to your partner's reactions with anger since you feel attacked. Doing so can imply that you are not taking responsibility for your actions and lack remorse—two misperceptions which will become a major obstacle to your partner's ability to move forward with you. Remember that this forgiveness process is a marathon and not a sprint. You may want to get past these issues as soon as possible, but real healing takes time. By being patient and understanding with your partner, you are showing your willingness to deal with a difficult issue, your understanding of how much this has hurt your partner, and your commitment to working things out in your relationship.

Additionally, practicing patience and understanding now will set you up for continually exhibiting these behaviors with your partner in the future. These qualities will be essential for your relationship even after you have worked through and repaired this current betrayal.

For Now, Avoid Explanation

From the beginning, you will want to explain the reasons for the affair. Your partner may even invite you, ask you, or beg you to tell them why you did this. Don't do it. Instead, say that the reasons it happened are not as important as the fact that it did, that you greatly regret the affair, and that no reasons can justify or defend your actions. It is a natural response to explain why you betrayed your partner, because you want them to know you are not a horrible person who wanted to hurt them. It is also natural for your partner to want information about how all of this happened to try to make sense of it. However, if you start explaining why you had the affair at the beginning of the healing process, most of the time, what you say will come across as a list of excuses and will sabotage your movement toward reconciliation.

If your partner insists on a discussion involving explanations of why you cheated, tread lightly and carefully. Tell him or her that you have some idea why you might have engaged in these behaviors, but that you need some time to figure more of it out before discussing it. Meeting with an individual therapist during this time would be an excellent idea, in part to help examine why you chose to take these actions. If your partner is aware that you are seeing a therapist during this time, they may be willing to delay these discussions about why because they know you are pursuing answers to these questions.

Truths and Tips to Hold On To

- ❖ As the betrayed, consider carefully which questions you really want answers to.

- ❖ As the betrayed, pull back from investigating further details about the affair if you find your thoughts keeping you awake or if you can't concentrate on life responsibilities.

- ❖ As the betrayed, acts of revenge may feel good in the short term. However, they may create difficulties for you in the future if you decide to move forward in your relationship.

- ❖ As the betrayer, telling the truth is of utmost importance if you wish to rebuild trust in your relationship.

- ❖ As the betrayer, remaining calm and listening are key indicators to your partner that you understand the pain your actions have caused and that you are committed to working things out.

- ❖ As the betrayer, do not offer your partner any explanations for your behavior at this early stage, since they will only sound like excuses.

- ❖ As the betrayer, seeing your own individual therapist to explore the reasons for your affair may not only help you find clarity, but also help your partner to be more patient about hearing explanations.

In the next chapter, we will explore the components of forgiveness.

CHAPTER 5

Forgiveness

As children, we are taught to say, "I'm sorry" and to forgive others when they hurt us. Religion also teaches us the benefits and morality of forgiveness. However, we often have misperceptions about what it means to forgive someone when they have hurt us significantly, such as in the case of having an affair. As you consider going through the process of forgiving your partner, here are some important aspects of forgiveness to keep in mind:

Forgiveness is Not . . .

The act of forgiveness is not a moral issue. Nor is it meant for the sake of doing the right thing or being morally superior to anyone else. "I will forgive you for this, but you owe me" is an approach that is not helpful. In fact, it can be quite destructive. A statement like this not only presents forgiveness as a favor with conditions, but also treats forgiveness as a decision that is immediately possible and merely subject to a person's will. Most of us know that forgiveness is not as easy as it sounds, especially following a significant betrayal. You may believe that you or your partner should forgive, but it is usually not possible to do so just when infidelity is first discovered. In fact, someone who tries to forgive too quickly might end up having to fake it, making this act into a burden they have to carry into the future. You may want to forgive or be forgiven quickly, in the hope that it will end your suffering. However, before this occurs, you and your partner must sufficiently deal with all of the issues involved. Without doing this, the relief you feel will be only temporary, and your relationship is not likely to succeed.

Forgiveness is also not amnesia.

Joe and Cindy went through couples counseling following the revelation that Joe had been having a year-long sexual relationship with his ex-girlfriend from high school. Joe and Cindy were both committed to staying together and were able to work through the process of forgiveness over the course of many months. Eventually, Cindy was able to forgive Joe for his affair. When this happened, both Cindy and Joe felt hopeful, relieved, and even more connected. Since then, however, Cindy feels a flood of emotions whenever she sees an affair play out on TV or when she drives by a restaurant where she knows Joe and the ex-girlfriend ate together. She often feels hurt and sad all over again about the affair.

When you decide to forgive your partner, you will not forget that the affair or betrayal happened. In fact, both partners will probably still have memories of the affair and how it affected them. Over time, you will probably think of these issues less often, but certain triggers are likely to bring emotions and memories back to the surface. You may want to forget and hope that by forgiving, you will erase the painful memories, but this does not happen. In fact, I believe it is better for both people occasionally to remember the affair, because this can serve as motivation to continually work on strengthening the relationship far beyond healing from the affair.

Forgiveness is also not an antidote for pain. The ability to forgive does not mean that you will be free from the hurt you feel. Over time, the pain you feel will be less intense. However, you may feel some level of sadness or anger for years into the future, even after you forgive your partner.

Finally, forgiveness is not saying to your partner that what they did is okay with you or that it was not a big deal. It was not okay and is never okay. Discussions through this process will help you and your partner understand the depth of pain that this affair has caused and how it has affected both of you. Often the person who has been betrayed is afraid to let go of their bitterness and let their partner out of the dog house, so to speak, because they fear it will send a false message that everything is back to normal or that what their partner did wasn't so bad. Believe it or not, you can both forgive your partner and hold them accountable at the same time.

Forgiveness is...

The start of forgiveness is acknowledging what your partner did to betray you, and how their behaviors emotionally impacted you. In addition, it is a chance to explore why the betrayal happened and make a choice to let go and move forward. Forgiveness includes saying to your partner that even though they hurt you immensely, you are willing and able to let go of your position as the hurt one and put your faith in them again. By forgiving, you are promising your partner that you will do your best to keep from punishing them for their affair behavior and hanging it over their head. Punishment can come in the form of sarcastic comments, verbal jabs, or even joking statements that come at the expense of your partner. These responses involve using the affair as a weapon of retaliation.

Months after Cindy has forgiven Joe for his affair, whenever their son Jared is struggling in school, Cindy wonders if the affair has affected him in a negative way and contributes now to his problems. Often when arguments about the children arise, she will blurt out, "If it weren't for your irresponsible and hurtful behavior with your ex, Jared wouldn't be having these difficulties!"

This type of outburst is an example of using the affair as a weapon and is a breach of trust on Cindy's part after she had promised to forgive.

Forgiveness also involves promising not to use the affair as justification for future behavior. For example, in the future, if your partner confronts you with behavior that they want you to change, you need to be careful not to respond with a statement like, "You can't bring these things up. What you did to me in the past by having an affair is so much worse than anything I have ever done!" Such an accusation is also a form of emotional blackmail that keeps the partner who had the affair at a constant disadvantage and excuses any wrongdoing on the betrayed partner's part.

Five years after the affair and forgiveness, Cindy starts to have lunch regularly with a male coworker, and never mentions these outings to Joe. One day, Joe drives by a restaurant and sees Cindy with another man. When he asks her about it later that night, Cindy becomes defensive and responds to his question with, "I wasn't doing anything wrong! You have no right even to ask me about this after what you did five years ago!"

Again, Cindy is using Joe's behavior during the affair to justify her actions now and she is going back on her promise to forgive him.

If you are not ready to let go of using the affair as a weapon or using it as a justification for your behaviors, you are not ready to forgive. Likewise, if you are not ready to put your trust in your partner, you are not ready to forgive. Remember, if either person's motivation for forgiveness is to run from the pain and just get on with the relationship, you also are probably not ready to forgive or be forgiven. Forgiveness is a choice, not a feeling. It is a decision to lay the past to rest as much as you can, and it is one you might have to make several times.

Truths and Tips to Hold On To

- Forgiveness is not a favor you do for your partner, saying that they owe you something in return.

- Forgiveness often takes time.

- Forgiveness is not forgetting that a betrayal has taken place.

- Forgiveness is not a guarantee that you won't feel pain, anger, shame, or guilt anymore.

- Forgiveness involves promising your partner that you will not punish them for their betrayal.

- Forgiveness is deciding not to use your partner's affair as an excuse for your own poor behaviors.

In the next chapter, I will describe an overview of the 4-Step Affair Recovery Process that I developed to guide couples through the important steps of forgiveness.

CHAPTER 6

Steps in the Forgiveness Process

To describe the process of forgiveness, I like to use the image of two people facing each other, holding hands. When you and your partner first became close, you probably felt some indescribable connection. This picture speaks to that connection. When an affair occurs in a relationship, it is as if a big earthquake causes a split in the ground and creates a chasm between you and your partner. Now you feel even further apart from each other than you might have felt before the affair, an experience that feels uncomfortable or even devastating. On the other hand, one of you may want more distance to create space for all of the unexpected emotions that have arisen between you.

If both of you want forgiveness to take place, you both must make an effort to bring the two cliffs closer together. Once you become closer, the individual who was hurt will then decide whether or not they are willing and able to take "a leap of faith" which will put them on the same ground as their partner. In a sense, the person who is taking the leap is recommitting their trust in the other person and the relationship. After this, I recommend that the couple participate in some kind of ceremony or ritual that represents the fact that both a significant hurt and forgiveness have occurred. The ceremony represents a new beginning or step in the relationship. In Chapter 10, I will offer some suggestions on how to make this event special and memorable.

Before you can begin the 4-Step Affair Recovery Process, you and your partner should discuss concrete ways to increase trust in the relationship. Lack of trust is the primary issue that causes the hurt; therefore, trust must be the first issue addressed. After a betrayal, it is critical that the couple take some steps to manage the crisis of lost trust. The person who has been betrayed feels anxious and unstable. They have been lied to in one way or another, and will therefore feel insecure, suspicious, and doubtful of their own ability to know when something is terribly wrong. As a result, they will have many questions and suspicions about new signs of betrayal. This chapter will help you choose some means of stabilizing this situation and beginning a new foundation of trust.

There are many practical steps that serve this purpose. For example, you can share passwords to accounts for email, voice mail, phones, and computers, as well as access to past and future cell phone and credit card records. Simply having the option to look at a cell phone or computer goes a long way toward removing the anxiety that secrecy causes. I have suggested to many couples that when home, they leave their phone or computer out rather than putting it away or keeping it on their person. Doing so creates a sense of transparency and openness that goes a long way toward correcting the breach of trust.

I also suggest that the person who had the affair provide abundant information about where they are going and whom they will be with in business or other situations. Regular check-ins by phone when away are also helpful. Each time the person who had the affair walks out the door, his or her partner has to deal with the fear of what might be happening when they are gone. Because of this, when possible, the betrayer should suspend some normal activities so that they are around their partner more. For example, the person may be able to work from home, take some time off, suspend business trips, exercise at home rather than at the gym, invite their partner to accompany them on errands, et cetera. These are just some of the ideas that serve the overall purpose of repairing broken trust and creating a sense of stability for the couple so that they can work on their relationship. It is important for both partners to suggest some of the methods they will use for this. When the betrayed offers suggestions, it gives them a sense of much-needed control. When the betrayer offers suggestions, they are taking responsibility for what has happened and showing a willingness to take care of it.

These behaviors to stabilize and increase trust won't have to last forever. However, some of them may be part of your ongoing effort to increase trust and openness in your relationship far beyond the time of forgiveness. Others will only be necessary at the beginning and during part of the healing process. You and your partner should always discuss changing your original agreement about these trust-building actions before you go back to the way things were before the affair. If you were the one to have the affair, I recommend you wait at least six months to a year after you have been forgiven to propose changing the agreements. In the meantime, be consistent with them and wait for your partner to take the lead if they would like to modify the agreement. This kind of patience will show your seriousness about the situation and empathy for your partner.

Resistance

Jose had an affair. He was actually relieved when his wife discovered it because of the stress and guilt he had been feeling. He ended the extramarital relationship, apologized many times, and wanted to work on his marriage. However, when his wife started demanding that she always know where he was, even questioning his short errands on weekends, he started to feel defensive and controlled. He even resisted giving her information or showing her his phone because he felt she was being unreasonable and that he did not deserve that kind of scrutiny.

If you have had an affair, you may be experiencing some discomfort about what you read above. I have heard the following comments: "I am telling the truth now, why doesn't she/he believe me?" "I feel like I am being treated like a child and someone is looking over my shoulder all the time." "I don't want the kind of relationship in which I have no privacy." "I am not doing anything wrong anymore, so why am I still being punished?" If your ultimate goal is to repair your relationship and have trust and connection long-term, this is a necessary part of the process. Your partner has this anxiety and needs this kind of access to information because of choices you have made. Remember, these accommodations and agreements do not need to last forever, but they are necessary following the discovery of an affair in order to get to the point of forgiveness and to re-establish trust.

If you want a relationship based on honesty and full disclosure, these commitments are of utmost importance. If you find yourself continually resisting, it may be that you actually do not want an open, transparent relationship. If this is the case, you need to discuss that reality with your partner so that you can both decide whether you want to stay together or not. A healthy relationship cannot be maintained if only one of the members wants full openness and disclosure.

There can also be resistance from the person who has been betrayed. Sometimes people resent feeling they have to spy or take

Steps in the Forgiveness Process

the time to find out whether their partner is still lying to them or not. Some feel that by taking these steps of looking at their partner's emails or phone calls, it puts them in the role of parent, which is not enjoyable at all. You need to do only what you feel comfortable doing. Just knowing that your partner is committing to your having the information may be all you need, even if you never choose to investigate. Again, this is short-term. If you both devote yourselves now to the recovery process, this will be something you do not have to think much or at all about in the future.

Having all of these strategies in place will not completely remove the stress and fear that something is still going on, but it will improve the sense of safety and security. There is no way to know for sure that you have all of the information or if your partner is being completely honest. This is the reality of the situation. However, without this improvement, it is difficult, if not impossible, to move on to the steps of forgiveness. Remember, all relationships involve trust and a level of risk, even relationships where there is no affair. You are just more acutely aware of this reality during the time following a significant betrayal.

After the agreements are in place to provide some stability and begin rebuilding trust, the 4-Step Affair Recovery Process can begin. The following is an outline and a brief description of this process. Each step is presented more thoroughly in the subsequent chapters. The initial three steps in this process are about moving the cliffs close enough for the last step of forgiveness to occur. The most important thing to keep in mind is that both partners need to be involved in this process to move them closer together. Each has a role to play and it is much more difficult, if not impossible, to do this alone.

The 4-Step Affair Recovery Process: A Brief Overview

The first step toward forgiveness is for you as a couple to explore and be clear about WHAT happened. In other words, besides the dishonesty about the affair relationship, what was the actual betrayal? The person betrayed has the right to know as many (or as few) of the details about the other relationship as they wish. Otherwise, it will be difficult to move forward in the process. Just as when you assemble a piece of furniture, it is a good idea to lay all of the components out before you, sharing as many facts as you can about the affair will add clarity to the situation and prepare you both to start rebuilding your relationship.

The second step in this process is EMPATHY. The goal here is to help the hurt individual feel that his or her partner really understands how this affair/betrayal has affected them. This step involves communicating feelings and emotions in the most constructive way possible.

The third step is the WHY step. The goal is for both parties to have a good contextual understanding of why the affair occurred. The objective is not to diminish your partner's responsibility, but to provide some answers to the question "Why did this happen?"

These initial three steps will help with healing and assist in bringing you closer together to prepare you for the fourth LEAP OF FAITH step. In this part of the process, the individual formally asks for forgiveness and their partner makes a commitment to forgive.

As I mentioned previously, after the four steps are completed, ideally the couple should create a ceremony or event that represents a new beginning in the relationship and a re-commitment to being faithful and to forgiving.

Steps in the Forgiveness Process

Although these steps are distinct in nature, they often overlap with one another as a couple moves through them. However, their order is of great importance. For example, if a couple tries to talk about the contextual understanding too soon, the discussion will seem like excuses that make the hurt individual feel as if their partner is not taking full responsibility for their actions. Also, if a couple does not put into place some agreements to address the trust issue before beginning the 4-Step Affair Recovery Process, they may continually be distracted by suspicions of inappropriate behaviors which will impact their ability to focus on the steps of empathy and contextual understanding. You will learn exactly how to build trust gradually in the remaining chapters of this book.

How long will all of this take? The answer depends upon the specific relationship and the individuals in the relationship. I highly recommend working with a couples therapist.

Recovering from betrayal is a difficult process with many potential landmines. It is easy to become derailed and give up. Working with a therapist will help keep you both on task since this trained, caring, and objective professional can help you manage the more difficult times. Expect that it will take between three and twelve months of continual work to go through these steps, depending upon the severity of the situation and your ability to communicate as a couple. If both partners are committed to the process and work diligently, the process will be smoother and faster.

Although the forgiveness process described in this book requires both partners to participate fully, it is still possible to forgive even if you are not going to stay together. If your relationship ends, you will have much more happiness and freedom as you move on if you are able to forgive. Of course, the process of reaching this type of forgiveness is not the subject of this book. Consult a good therapist or counselor if this is your situation.

Truths and Tips to Hold On To

- Before you can begin the 4-Step Affair Recovery Process, reestablishing trust as a couple is key.

- Ways to reestablish trust include sharing passwords to computers and phones, sharing details about your whereabouts and the people you are with, spending more time at home, and suspending business trips.

- The trust-building agreements you establish with your partner should last at least 6–12 months before you discuss changing them.

- Step One in the forgiveness process involves sharing as much information as you can about the facts of the affair.

- Step Two is about developing empathy by communicating feelings honestly and constructively.

- Step Three establishes contextual understanding about the betrayal and answers the question "Why did this happen?"

- Step Four is called The Leap of Faith and requires the betrayer to ask for forgiveness and the betrayed to commit to forgiving.

Now that you have an overview of what it will take as a couple and as individuals to work through my 4-Step Affair Recovery Process, you are ready to take the first step of discussing what happened in the affair.

CHAPTER 7

Step 1: What Actually Happened?

The person involved in the affair is obviously aware of exactly what happened. However, most of the time, their partner is not. In the beginning, the only information that the partner knows is from their own discovery or what they have heard from others. Although there are times when a person having an affair will tell their partner about it, more often it comes as a horrible surprise. Often the betrayer denies it and then eventually may confess some information about what happened in the affair. Over time, after a lot of questioning, more and more information may emerge.

The person involved in the affair needs to be as transparent as possible as early as possible in the process of healing and forgiveness. Most will resist this because they are ashamed of their behaviors, worry about their partner's reaction, and don't want to hurt their partner more by providing details. However, the longer it takes to convey the information, the more difficult it will be to rebuild trust and heal the relationship.

In my work, I ask the betrayer to write the story of the entire affair from start to finish. They need to write it in a timeline format and be as detailed as possible. I will also ask the betrayed to write down any unanswered questions about what happened. In the next session, the betrayer will read the story while their partner listens, and then the betrayed will have an opportunity to ask any follow-up questions.

Two things are important to remember when working on Step One. First, the betrayed individual should be able to have absolutely any questions answered about the facts of what happened between their partner and the other person. Remember, whatever the individual does not disclose is still a secret and will interfere with the healing process as well as the goal of a loving, connected, trusting, open relationship.

One caveat: The questions you ask at this time should deal with the facts, not the feelings involved in the affair. Questions about how good it felt to sleep with the other person or whether your partner found the other person more attractive are not helpful for healing and will only feed your own feelings of insecurity and hurt. They can also feel accusatory toward the betrayer and hinder further openness. Even though these types of questions are difficult to talk about, they can be addressed in Step Three when you discuss the context of the affair.

Second, there may be factual information that the betrayed might not want to know about the details of the affair. This individual needs to weigh the costs and benefits of knowing these details before asking for this information. The benefits might include having more concrete facts. Knowing facts can help prevent the person from imagining other scenarios. The costs of knowing details can include pictures in their mind of their partner with another individual that might be very disturbing and difficult to forget. These images may stay with them for many years and may inhibit their ability to forgive and move beyond the affair. The betrayed should always be cognizant of how the information they ask for might help or hurt them in the process of repairing the relationship, even though they have a right to know about any part of the affair they wish.

Step 1: What Actually Happened?

The goal of this step is not only to be clear on the specifics regarding the affair, but also to form an agreement on what parts of this relationship were betrayals to their primary relationship contract. The entire outside relationship may have been a betrayal, or only the parts that have been kept a secret. This step will help you both review what the contract was (and is), as well as in what ways the betrayer broke that contract. The betrayal may include talking with another person while keeping it secret from their partner, looking at pornography on the internet or having sexual contact with another person. Generally, it is any behavior or action that the betrayer intentionally kept from their partner. It almost always includes lying by commission (i.e., telling someone something you know is not true) or omission (i.e., keeping information from another person that you know that person would want to know). These are examples of the parts of the betrayal that need to be forgiven. Once you as a couple agree clearly about these things, you are ready for Step 2 of the forgiveness process.

Many couples have never explicitly defined these types of relationship boundaries before. At this point in the process, if you disagree on whether a specific behavior signifies a breach of trust, try not to fall into debating about it. Instead, for now, focus on the behaviors you do agree were betrayals and then, following the process of forgiveness, get more clear about what boundaries you agree upon moving forward.

The Shame Effect

If you've had an affair, most likely you have experienced deep levels of shame at some point. Shame occurs because our self-worth can be so intricately linked to our behavior. Often, a person who has taken part in betrayal behaviors not only recognizes their cheating actions, but also regards themselves as a cheater. Since being a cheater may mean that you feel unworthy of love, you may wish to deny some of the facts that would further prove this idea of being unlovable.

However, this reluctance to tell the whole truth will only worsen the problem, since shame only grows in secrecy. By shining light on the facts of what happened, you are building up what Brené Brown calls your *shame resilience*, and growing in the vulnerability you and your partner will need in order to heal. I will discuss shame resilience even more in Step 4. For now, sharing your shame with a therapist or close friend can help you shed significant light on it to keep it from growing even more.

Step 1: What Actually Happened?

Truths and Tips to Hold On To

❖ The betrayer needs to be as transparent as possible about the facts involved in the affair, even if they worry about hurting their partner further.

❖ The betrayed has the right to ask any questions about what happened but should wait to ask questions about their partner's feelings around the affair until dealing with the context of the affair in Step Three.

❖ Both partners should discuss what parts of the affair were actual betrayals of their contract—which, in general, is any behavior or information the betrayer intentionally kept from their partner.

❖ Once you have completed the 4-Step Affair Recovery Process, you and your partner should get clear on what the boundaries of your relationship need to be from now on.

❖ For the betrayer, shame about your behaviors can often make you feel unlovable, making you reluctant to tell the entire truth.

❖ Building shame resilience by choosing to continue to be vulnerable ultimately will help you and your partner heal.

The next chapter will describe Step Two of the 4-Step Affair Recovery Process at great length. Please take your time with all of the materials in this chapter, since its topic, developing empathy, is key to moving on successfully to the last two steps.

CHAPTER 8

Step 2: Empathy for the Betrayed

The next step of the 4-step process will encourage feelings of empathy for the betrayed individual. Both partners in the relationship need to spend time and energy on this crucial part of repair. The goal is for you as the betrayer to feel real empathy for your partner, and for you as the betrayed to know that you are understood.

Empathy is sharing emotions or an experience of another person to the point that you can feel at least some of what they are feeling. When I work with couples using the 4-Step Affair Recovery Process, I assign them homework that I recommend they begin working on as soon as possible after the session in which we discuss what actually happened in the affair. The assignment is for both individuals to write down, from their perspectives, the list of emotions that the betrayed individual has experienced as a result of the affair. After recording these emotions, they then go back to each of the feeling words and explain their own definition of this emotion. Beginning this assignment soon after the disclosure session will assist them because those feelings will be stirred up during the session and will be closer to the surface of awareness. I then ask the couple to bring what they have written down to their next session so we can read and process it. During this session, the betrayed individual begins by reading and describing their emotional reactions to the affair in a slow and methodical way while their partner is listening carefully. Then the person who had the affair talks about what stood out for them from what their partner shared.

Now it is their turn to read the list they brought to the session. When reading each feeling, I check with the betrayed partner to see if these emotions match their experience.

Another way to understand this process is to imagine looking at a painting, and trying to describe all the details of the painting to someone else. The colors and images of the painting represent the emotions present as a result of an affair. If you are the one who has been betrayed, you need to explain the complexities of this painting to yourself and to your partner. The better your partner is able to listen and reflect back to you the details of the painting, the more you will feel understood. Here are some examples of feeling statements that have come up for couples I've worked with:

- "I felt hurt."
- "I can't believe you are my best friend and you did this."
- "I can feel it in my bones. I feel afraid this might be the end and what that means for our children."
- "I feel so sad, I don't know if I'll ever get over this."

Write all of the emotions you have experienced as a result of the affair. This exercise is about you and your own pain that needs to be voiced in order to heal.

For an empathic exchange, the following elements are necessary:

1. The betrayed's ability to describe clearly how they feel.
2. The betrayer's openness of heart and mind to listen and connect with what is communicated.
3. The betrayer's ability to convey that they deeply understand the emotions that were experienced by their partner.

Step 2: Empathy for the Betrayed

A note on this last element: There are ways to convey empathy without using words, depending on what you know about your partner. For example, you may know that they would love an affectionate embrace after sharing their feelings. On the other hand, if you are aware that your partner usually needs physical space when strong emotions arise, you may choose not to cuddle at all. In both cases, even though the behaviors seem to be each other's opposites, you are showing empathy.

As the betrayed, being able to express your feelings will take time and insight into your emotions so that you can find the words to describe them to your partner. Examining these emotions will be painful, so it is important to pace yourself. You won't be able to do this in one day. I recommend that you spend a limited period of time each day thinking, processing, and writing about your emotions. Again, do not spend all day doing this, just a set amount of time. You may want to carry a notepad or write feelings down in your phone in case some emotions or insights arise during the day. Then, even if you are doing something like shopping for groceries and a feeling comes, you can spend some time in the grocery store parking lot documenting this information so that you can share it with your partner later. You may find yourself resisting even thinking about the affair or its effects because of the pain involved, but it is a necessary part of the healing process. If you become overwhelmed, take a break. Keep in mind that this step can last weeks or even months before you have a full understanding of the affair's impact on you.

What follows is a list of emotions that are commonly experienced by the betrayed individual after an affair has surfaced. Their descriptions may help you understand your own experience and then be able to express it to your partner. You may feel some or all of these emotions at any given time in the process.

Shock

You might be in shock when you learn that your partner has betrayed you. This may include numbness or an inability to focus or think about anything other than the affair. When people are in shock, the sensation can feel like an out-of-body experience. This is known as a dissociative state, and it is considered to be an involuntary coping mechanism. When your body is flooded with difficult feelings, your psyche creates a dreamlike sensation to effect a break from the level of trauma you are experiencing.

Surprise

Often, one of the first emotions someone experiences when they discover their partner has been unfaithful is surprise. If you are like many people, you may never have imagined that this could happen to you. You may have discovered information over time, and all along the way, kept hoping that it was not true. As the reality of your situation sinks in, the next emotion may very well be anger.

Anger

As you begin to deal with the aftermath of an affair, you may only be able to identify anger or rage towards your partner and the situation. However, over time, you will be able to understand the myriad of other emotions behind this anger.

Pain

One obvious feeling that arises is pain. Some thoughts that may accompany these feelings include the following: *How can this person who supposedly cares about me have betrayed me this way? I opened myself up to this person in an emotional and physical way and now he or she has broken my trust. I feel so disrespected.* Whenever someone becomes vulnerable to another person, they risk feeling hurt. It is natural to experience this following the realization that your partner was unfaithful and lied to you.

Guardedness

When someone feels hurt and vulnerable, they often want to protect themselves from getting hurt again and will begin to guard themselves by withholding thoughts and feelings. Following an affair, this can lead to shutting down emotions, pulling away, and putting up walls.

Disappointment

People often feel disappointed in their partner when they learn their partner cheated on them. They may have admired their partner and now see them in a different light. Their expectations have not been met, and they must now reconcile their old way of seeing their partner with what's happened.

Anxiety

Another common feeling is anxiety. What you thought to be true is not true. You thought your partner would never do this, but he or she did. You are asking, "How could this have happened?" You may question your judgment and whether or not your partner is really who you thought he or she was. You may say to yourself, "I thought my partner was a person with integrity and ethics—but maybe they are not," or "How can a person with integrity and ethics lie and cheat in a relationship?" You may feel anxiety both about what has happened, as well as fear that this will happen again.

Most people also feel anxiety about the future of the relationship. They are full of questions, such as, "Is this the end of our relationship?" or "If we stay together, will I ever be able to trust my partner again?" Whether you stay together or break up, the future seems unstable. If you have children, you naturally feel worried about how all of this will affect them.

Insecurity

You may also feel anxious because you doubt your own intuition. If you were not aware of the fact that your spouse was being unfaithful, how can you trust your ability to protect yourself from this situation in the future? In the past, you may have developed a trust in your sense of reality and now you feel you cannot even trust yourself. If you can't trust yourself, then whom can you trust? People in the world may all of a sudden seem more mysterious and uncertain. Remember, anxiety is the result of uncertainty, and you probably feel very uncertain about life and your future at this point.

You may also feel insecure about yourself as a person. You may ask yourself, "If I was such a wonderful person, why would my partner have chosen to be with someone else?" or "What is defective or wrong with me that caused my partner to be with someone else?"

Unattractiveness

"What was it about me that wasn't good enough or attractive enough for my partner to be satisfied and not look outside our relationship?"

Step 2: Empathy for the Betrayed

You may get to the point of asking this question to yourself or even asking your partner. The affair might shake your self-esteem and self-confidence, and you might start doubting how attractive you are either physically or otherwise. If you do feel this way, it is important to explain this to your partner in order for them to have a sense of how their behavior affected you. However, usually affairs are not about how attractive or unattractive you are to your spouse. Even beautiful movie stars experience betrayal in their relationships. The reasons people have affairs are complex, and we will examine them more in the next chapter.

Unsettledness

This is the feeling that comes when what you thought was true and real ends up not being true at all. People who have been cheated on may feel unsettled about the way they saw their relationship prior to the affair. They may also feel unsettled about how this is going to affect their relationship moving forward or even whether their relationship will survive this crisis. Additionally, they may feel as if they have never known their partner, now that their partner has cheated. Lastly, they may be unsettled about what their future looks like, with or without their partner. These worries and concerns can all contribute to the unsettled feeling following the discovery of an affair.

Craziness

Because of all the emotions you are feeling, you may feel and even act a bit crazy at times, like you are losing your mind or having a nervous breakdown. You may experience some level of paranoia, believing that you can't trust anything about your partner and maybe even other people. Your mind may go off to wild ideas about what you still don't know or what could happen as a result of this affair. You may analyze again and again past experiences or situations in your relationship in an attempt to make sense of it all. When you do all of this, you might step back and take a look at yourself and feel as if you are going crazy.

Sadness

You probably feel sad or depressed about the state of your life and relationship right now. It might be difficult to enjoy anything or even get out of bed. Some people lose their appetite, and feel sick to their stomachs if they think about eating. Additionally, you might feel sadness or grief if you worry that your relationship or your family may not stay together. If you anticipate a breakup or divorce, you know it will affect your children and the rest of your family, as well as your social support system.

Loss of Innocence or Purity

Part of your sadness may stem from the loss of innocence in your relationship. Even though you or your partner may have been involved in other relationships before being with each other, you may have had this vision of purity moving forward: that you and your partner had something with each other that no one else was a part of. Following an affair, your relationship might feel contaminated. Your partner shared certain things emotionally or physically with another person that were only supposed to be shared with you. This can be intensified if you know this person, or if your partner was with this other person in your car or home. These situations can lead to a greater feeling of violation. Not only has this other person contaminated your relationship; it might feel that they have contaminated your home, car, or neighborhood.

Grief

This affair might feel like a death. You lost your relationship as it was or as you believed it was. You might lose your relationship, your family, your community, your future together, etc. This can all feel like a form of death and loss to you.

Unappreciated

People often feel unappreciated when they discover their partner has betrayed them with someone else. This happens often if they are committed primarily to raising the children or financially supporting the family. If they are doing their part for the family and their partner is spending time and energy with another person outside their relationship and family during this time, they may not feel appreciated for all of their efforts to contribute to the relationship and family.

Disrespect

You may feel disrespected by your partner's unfaithfulness. Respect implies thinking highly of or having admiration for someone. You may be thinking that if your partner really respected you, they would not have violated your trust. You might say to yourself, "If my partner really had respect for me, they would have had the guts to talk to me about their unhappiness with our relationship before this happened. But instead, it feels like they took the easy route and had an affair." When a partner has an affair, it may feel like the ultimate sign of disrespect.

Embarrassment or Shame

Many people feel embarrassed or ashamed following an affair. Depending upon who is aware of the affair and how much information they know, it may feel like your dirty laundry is out in the open for everyone to see. You might worry that other people will wonder what was wrong with you to make your partner cheat, or you might worry that people see you and your partner as damaged goods and want to stay away from you. You might think that your family or friends will look down on you for deciding to stay with someone who hurt you this way. If you feel this emotion strongly, it might even affect your ability or desire to work on healing the relationship.

Disgust

Depending upon what type of affair your partner has had, you certainly could be experiencing disgust, especially if the affair included a sexual component. Another individual has been involved with your partner in a very intimate way, and the affair very well may have taken place between times that the two of you were intimate. Having this knowledge or the visualizations of these sexual acts may contribute to feelings of disgust.

Confusion

All of the following questions are very normal to ask during this time and indicate the feeling of confusion.

- "Why did this happen?"
- "What actually did happen?"
- "How could this have happened?"
- "When could this have happened?"
- "Why didn't I see this coming?"
- "What does this mean for our family's future?"
- "What should I do now?"
- "What will people think?"

- "Does my partner really care about me?"
- "Will my partner ever cheat again?"
- "Will I ever be able to trust either my partner or someone else again?"

Abandonment/Aloneness

You may feel that your partner abandoned you and possibly your children by choosing to be with someone else. In a sense, they gave up time with you and energy toward only you, and focused on someone else during periods of time. When people feel abandoned, they often feel alone. Even if other people are aware of the relationship crisis of an affair, it may still feel as though you are in it by yourself.

Frustration

You might feel frustrated in a number of different ways about your partner having had an affair. You might feel frustrated right after the discovery that your partner behaved in this way instead of making different decisions such as talking with you about their unhappiness or going to couples counseling. If you and your partner decide to attempt the repair process following an affair, you might at times feel frustrated that things are not moving along faster in the healing process. You may feel frustrated that you continue to experience so many of these difficult emotions or because your partner doesn't seem to be doing everything they can to repair this betrayal.

Hopelessness

All of the above emotions can eventually lead to feelings of hopelessness—one of the most difficult emotions to face. If you are feeling hopeless, know that this is normal in your situation and that levels of it may fluctuate. Also remember that no matter what happens now and in the future, you can be okay and potentially go on to live a happy, healthy life.

Remember that you may feel all or some of the emotions listed in this chapter at different times and at different levels. You probably also feel some emotions that are not even listed. In no way is this list meant to be exhaustive. All of your feelings and emotions are valid and need to be explored and acknowledged. Understanding your feelings will be an important step in the forgiveness process before you can even explain them to your partner. It is also important for your partner to listen to you and be open to how their actions have emotionally affected you. Remember, you are painting. Just as in a picture one might see many different shades of the color blue, you will have emotions that are complex and variable, and need to be explained in detail if your partner is going to be able to understand fully the effect that their behaviors have had on you.

If you are the one who betrayed your partner, it is important to be as empathetic as possible. Empathy involves both connecting emotionally with your partner's feelings and also demonstrating this understanding through your words and actions. You might find it difficult opening yourself to really hearing how you have affected your partner. You may still care very much for them and not want them to suffer because of you. You may also find yourself getting defensive when your partner tells you how they feel because you, in turn, feel attacked. It is important to manage your emotions and remain as calm, open, and patient as possible when working on empathy. If you are finding it difficult, it is wise to find a trusted therapist to assist you in this process.

Let's revisit our couples from Chapter 2 to discover their emotional reactions when affairs are discovered. Please note the bolded areas that highlight the emotions.

Step 2: Empathy for the Betrayed

Story #1: Marjorie and Devon

Devon's Emotional Response to Marjorie's Affair with a Coworker

*When Devon found out about Marjorie's affair, he felt **shocked, angry, hurt, disappointed, insecure, sad, embarrassed, and disgusted**. He was **shocked** because he never, ever thought Marjorie could do something like this. She had always been an ethical person and would actually talk negatively about people who cheated on their spouses. Devon is **angry** that she could do this to him and the family in light of all of the possible consequences of her behaviors. He is **hurt**. It is not easy for him to open up to other people, and he was vulnerable with Marjorie and relied on her. He is **disappointed** that she chose to behave this way. It seems totally out of character for her and the way she was raised. Devon feels **insecure**. He is a stay-at-home dad and if this event ends their relationship, will he and the kids be okay? He is **sad** for himself and the kids. Will this mean the end of their relationship and the end of their family being all together? He is **embarrassed** about the situation because everyone in their community seems to admire their relationship and if other people found out about this, they may think differently about him, Marjorie, and their family. Devon also feels **disgusted** when he sees images of Marjorie and this other guy being intimate together in his mind. Devon has many other emotions and eventually is able to communicate them to Marjorie.*

Story #2: Sherry and Abraham

Abraham's Emotional Response to Sherry's Affair with Manuel

*When Abraham found out about this situation, he felt **angry, hurt, disappointed, disrespected, disgusted, frustrated, hopeless and unappreciated**. He feels **angry** that his wife was spending so much* time with another man and was physical with him. He feels **hurt** that she would do something like this to him after he was always faithful to her. He feels **disappointed** that Sherry would engage in these behaviors and wonders if he ever knew the real Sherry. He feels **disrespected** by Sherry's engaging in behaviors with another man while he was working to support the family. He feels **disgusted** when he thinks about Sherry and the other guy spending time together and being physically intimate with each other. He feels **frustrated** that she didn't talk with him first and initiate couples counseling before she chose to get involved with the guy. He feels **hopeless** that he may never be able to forgive her and that their relationship might be tarnished forever. He feels **unappreciated** for having worked so hard to create a life and financial security for Sherry and the family while she was spending her time and energy thinking about and developing a relationship with another man. Abraham also has many other emotions about this affair and eventually is able to communicate them to Sherry both in and out of therapy.

Story #3: Steve and Jessica

<u>Jessica's Emotional Response to Steve's Affair with Multiple Women</u>

When Jessica found out about this situation, she felt **shocked, hurt, guarded, confused, disgusted, abandoned, unattractive and hopeless.** She feels **shocked** because of the length of time and frequency of these behaviors. She feels **hurt** that Steve didn't disclose some of the behaviors earlier in their relationship so she would know what she was getting into, and they could perhaps have addressed them together. She feels **guarded** now because she feels she can't trust anything about Steve, so she has to be careful not to get hurt anymore. She feels **confused** about why Steve would do all of this when they had such an active and seemingly enjoyable physical relationship. She feels **disgusted** when

Step 2: Empathy for the Betrayed

*imagining Steve's behaviors with other women. She feels **abandoned** by him when she recalls him having said he was moving toward her in order to get married and live a life together. She feels **unattractive** when she compares herself to escorts and women in pornography. She feels **hopeless**. Can Steve ever stop engaging in these long-time behaviors? If he can't, will they ever make it together? Along with conveying these emotions and doubts, Jessica talks with Steve about many other feelings she has been experiencing after finding out about Steve's behaviors over the years.*

Hopefully, after talking through their emotions, the betrayed person will feel empathy from their partner. At this point, I often ask the betrayed person how much empathy they feel from their partner for their emotions about the affair. I even suggest giving a number or percentage of how much empathy they feel on a scale from 0 to 85%. I do not believe anyone can truly know 100% of how another experiences an event like an affair because we are all so different. Usually, the answer to this question at this point is somewhere in the 30%–50% range. You should continue to increase this sense of empathy to about 70–75% before you move on to the next step in the forgiveness process. Remember, if a couple moves too quickly to Step 3 and starts discussing why the affair occurred before the empathy amount is high enough, the discussion may feel like excuses for the affair rather than an exploration of why it happened.

Therefore, we continue our exploration of empathy by asking the question: What demonstrates empathy and what demonstrates a lack of empathy? I often explore this question thoroughly with couples at this stage of the forgiveness process because, to some extent, empathy is in the eye of the beholder. The betrayer might want to try to demonstrate empathy but might be missing the mark, so that the betrayed individual still doesn't perceive the empathy.

Actions that Demonstrate Empathy

- Listening to your partner by looking at them and actively nodding your head or having an open expression on your face.

- Saying things like, "It makes sense that you feel this way," "I can absolutely understand why you would feel this way" or "I'm so sorry" with soft compassion.

- Checking in with your partner regularly (maybe even daily at the beginning) and directly about how they are feeling about the affair and your relationship. This act can be one of the most difficult things to do, but also one of the most powerful behaviors to show empathy because it shows you are recognizing the significant trauma the affair has caused and are willing to sit with your partner in their pain.

- Being patient with your partner. They will need to ask a lot of questions, often more than once. They may need to process how they are feeling over and over and over again. They will not always believe you when you answer their questions. Their emotions will continue to be triggered by different thoughts or events, possibly for quite a long time. You may be feeling that things are getting better between you, and then your partner may have a bad day. Patience is a must; empathy cannot happen without it.

- Being willing to be open with your partner about all of your accounts, passwords, etc., as well as where you are and what you are doing day and night.

- Cutting off all communication and staying away from the person in the affair. This might even include leaving your job if this person works with you, or leaving your neighborhood if this person lives near you.
- Taking time off work or traveling less for work.
- Being emotionally open to your partner's feelings but also open with your own feelings. Your feelings should not take precedence over your partner's feelings, but if you are feeling guilty or heartbroken about how your behavior has affected your partner, find opportunities to share these emotions.

Actions that Demonstrate a Lack of Empathy

- Getting frustrated with your partner for wanting to talk about the affair or asking a lot of questions. This might be communicated verbally through your words or nonverbally through your actions or facial expressions.
- Getting defensive when talking about the affair or making excuses for why you had it. This might include talking about why you did what you did or mentioning things you were unhappy about in your relationship.
- Saying things like, "How long do we have to keep talking about this?" or "How long do we need to continue to go to counseling about this?" or "I thought we were beyond this." All of these statements minimize the impact this has had on your partner and send the message to them to *get over it* more quickly.

- Demonstrating non-verbal responses such as sighing or rolling your eyes when your partner mentions the affair.

- Focusing too much on your own feelings about the affair. This can include how much you miss the other person or how sad you feel about ending the relationship. It can also include self-loathing or martyrdom such as, "I'm a horrible, horrible person who deserves to be punished as much as possible" or "I don't deserve to be forgiven because my behaviors are unforgivable." These types of statements can come across as selfish and self-centered at a time when you need to be attentive to your partner. If you have these emotions, it would be best to talk with your individual therapist about them, not your partner.

- Pursuing your partner physically or sexually. Sometimes couples will connect physically or sexually even while they are in the midst of repairing from an affair. Others feel the need to avoid physical contact altogether. You will need to take your cues from your partner about what they need in this arena and what they are comfortable with. Remember, be patient.

In addition to the above examples, there are more ways to demonstrate empathy or a lack of it. Couples need to communicate about this either by themselves or with help from a couples counselor to give the betrayer a road map for how to increase their level of empathy for the betrayed.

If you and your partner have spent time exploring these emotions and the impact the affair has had on you, and you now feel a significant amount of empathy from your partner (maybe 70%–85%), it may be time to start exploring why the affair happened in the first place. If you feel understood, you can explore the reasons for the affair without those reasons feeling like they are merely excuses.

Think of the next step of the forgiveness process as increasing the contextual understanding of the affair. This will be important for the one who had the affair, as well as for their partner. For the betrayer, without understanding the past, it is difficult to learn from your mistakes and make different choices in the future. For the betrayed, by understanding better what led your partner down the path of an affair, you can hopefully have some empathy for them and be more able to extend grace and forgiveness to them. For both partners, exploring the contextual part of the affair will heighten your awareness of signs of trouble to look out for in the future. Without an understanding of how your relationship arrived at this point and how the individual arrived at the point of having an affair, you are at risk of getting back into the same situation.

The Shame Effect

According to Brené Brown, shame causes people to feel *"trapped, powerless, and isolated."* These unpleasant emotions cause most people to adopt what Brown calls *shame shields*—strategies of disconnection that move people either away from, against, or toward other people.

In the case of an affair, some examples of shame shields that may move you away from your partner include secret keeping, changing the subject, ignoring, isolating yourself, and disappearing into life responsibilities. Alternatively, shame shields that can move you against your partner involve fighting back by trying to shame them, and include sarcasm, lashing out, and blaming. Finally, shame shields that can move you toward your partner involve people pleasing, gift giving, controlling the way they see you, and apologizing when you are not really sorry. Take a moment to think about your own shame shields and what may trigger them.

Recognizing some of the unhealthy ways you may deal with your shame is the first step to handling shame. Facing shame head on is crucial if you and your partner want to reestablish trust through authentic conversations and honesty.

Step 2: Empathy for the Betrayed

Truths and Tips to Hold On To

- ❖ For the betrayer, true empathy involves listening to your partner's feelings and being able to reflect them clearly and thoughtfully.

- ❖ For the betrayed, describing your emotions to your partner in as much detail as possible will help you feel better understood so that you can eventually heal from your pain.

- ❖ Common emotions that come up for the betrayed partner include shock, anger, disappointment, anxiety, sadness, and grief. These are all normal.

- ❖ For the betrayer, developing increasing empathy is important before moving on to the next step in the forgiveness process when you will discuss the reasons why the affair happened. Otherwise, if your partner doesn't feel understood, they are likely to perceive these reasons as excuses for your behaviors.

- ❖ For the betrayer, showing empathy may include actively nodding when listening to your partner, being willing to share passwords to devices, saying phrases like "I'm so sorry," and being patient with your partner when they repeatedly ask questions.

- ❖ Conversely, certain behaviors such as getting frustrated, rolling your eyes, sighing, sharing too much about your own feelings, and pursuing your partner physically or sexually can show a lack of empathy.

- ❖ As the betrayer, the shame you feel about your affair may cause you to develop shame shields, which are strategies of disconnection and self-protection.

- ❖ Recognizing these shame shields that can move you against, away from, or toward your partner in unhealthy ways will help you to stay honest and vulnerable in your conversations.

Once you and your partner feel you have built up enough empathy by listening to the betrayed's emotions, you will be ready to continue to Step 3 in the next chapter.

CHAPTER 9

Step 3: Understanding Why the Affair Occurred

Why did this happen? This is one of the most important and pressing questions following an affair. Certainly the partner in the relationship who is hurt by the affair will ask this question many times throughout the process, but even the person who participated in the betrayal may wonder about this. Often the simple answer is that the person wanted to feel good sexually or get attention from another person. Although this may be true, it is important to understand the layers beyond just the simple answer in order to make sense of it and hopefully keep it from happening again.

As I've said before, every individual is ultimately responsible for the choices they make in life. This is true when someone chooses to keep secrets from their partner and when they decide to engage in a relationship outside their primary one. However, it is helpful to examine how the person who had the affair got there. Affairs usually don't happen instantaneously or spontaneously. In general, they develop over time and involve a series of decisions. As you read further in this chapter, remember that giving reasons for a behavior is not the same thing as making excuses for it. It is also important not to discuss Step 3 before establishing a significant amount of empathy in Step 2. If a couple begins to explore the reasons why someone had an affair too soon, this conversation will quickly feel like excuses, not reasons, for the affair. Of course, this may set the couple back in their process of forgiveness.

Some Common Factors that Can Lead to an Affair

Unfulfilled Primary Relationship

Most people assume that unsatisfying relationships are at least one of the reasons for affairs. Some couples engage in regular conflict, while others simply experience physical or emotional disconnection.

If your relationship is filled with destructive conflict, you may start wanting to spend more and more time away from your partner to avoid the conflict. This can include staying at work longer hours or getting more involved in outside interests or hobbies. This absence can lead to more conflict in your relationship and then to more avoidance. During this time, other relationships can develop outside of your primary one that may seem much more fulfilling and peaceful. For example, you may start talking to your coworker or tennis teammate about your primary relationship, and use them as a sounding board. This can create a sense of closeness for both parties and send signals that you are interested in having another relationship outside your primary, conflict-ridden relationship.

You may feel you are justified in staying away from home because of how much strife and unhappiness exist there and may even feel that crossing the line into another relationship is justified because of how badly your partner treats you. You might even tell yourself that your partner probably will not care about your cheating behaviors because he or she does not care much about you. In addition, maybe you feel that your relationship is over, so it does not matter what you do with another individual.

If you feel alienated in your primary relationship, you may long for connection with someone. Maybe you feel that you have tried to

Step 3: Understanding Why the Affair Occurred

talk with your partner about this disconnected feeling and that you were ignored or dismissed. Another person who comes into your life and seems to enjoy talking to you, spending time with you, or wants to be in a physical relationship with you, can feel very enticing. Betrayal often starts with small conversations that seem innocent, then some flirtatious behavior until finally a line is crossed. This line can seem fuzzy, and when you are in the middle of the process, you might not even be aware you are in a danger zone until a clear line (e.g., sexual contact) has been crossed. By that time, you may already feel attached to the person (or what this person represents), and have a difficult time disengaging from him or her. In addition, you may feel guilty because you know that on some level you are not living with integrity. Some people use alcohol or drugs to numb this guilt, or continually tell themselves that their partner will never know and that "what they don't know can't really hurt them."

It should go without saying that the weaker the primary relationship, the more susceptible it is to outside influences and temptations. While I'm not suggesting that the partner of the person who had the affair is in any way responsible or at fault for the affair, understanding what was missing in a relationship gives clarity to how an affair evolved and can possibly keep a future affair from happening. If a couple identifies areas of difficulty in their relationship that contributed to the discontent, they can work on addressing these areas and strengthening their relationship. This type of clarity can potentially ensure that affairs are much less likely to occur in the future.

Depression or General Unhappiness

Many people who are unfaithful to their partners are unhappy during the time the affair is developing. They may be unhappy with more than just their primary relationship. In fact, their primary relationship might not even be especially bad. Often life circumstances such as clinical depression, difficulty at work, financial strain, or the burden of stay-at-home parenting are the causes of unhappiness. Sometimes if a person has been suffering from an illness or injury, or feels unhappy about getting older, they will feel dissatisfied with their circumstances and start to look for a distraction. They might want to feel stronger, healthier, or younger and look to an affair to fulfill that desire. The outside relationship can be a way to distract themselves or escape from unhappiness and live in an alternate world in which everything is new, exciting, low-stress and generally okay. Sometimes people are not even aware of how unhappy they are until they end up in an affair and cause significant damage to their primary relationship.

Alcohol and Drugs

Alcohol and drugs work in a few different ways to influence a person to cheat. First, they can be a way to temporarily escape the realities and stressors of life by helping someone to tune out. A partner can respond to this behavior by trying to manage it, saying things such as, "You shouldn't drink so much." This can cause the person to withdraw even further, in an attempt to avoid feeling controlled or scolded. Or they can resist the control and try to rebel by consuming even more alcohol or drugs.

Second, consumption of alcohol and drugs might lead to behaviors that strain a relationship, such as staying out late at night, not responding when your partner is looking for you, or behaving in an embarrassing or inappropriate way around your partner. If the other partner does not engage in the same behaviors, the couple may find

Step 3: Understanding Why the Affair Occurred

themselves with two separate social circles that will exacerbate their feelings of disconnection.

A third way that alcohol and drugs may cause disloyal behaviors is that people are not as thoughtful about the consequences of their actions when they are impaired. Most people are not at their best and do not make wise decisions when consuming drugs or alcohol. Getting drunk or high shuts down your frontal lobe—the part of your brain that helps you make rational decisions. This impairment can lead to problems with boundaries with others and to making unhealthy choices.

Insecurities

Many people are insecure about their own attractiveness or value. This can make them especially vulnerable to getting into an affair when they receive attention or compliments from another person. Receiving very little positive feedback, or worse, a lot of criticism at home from your partner, can lead to even more yearning for someone to admire and compliment you. This new relationship can start off innocently but quickly become intoxicating if you feel as if you are starving for attention or value.

Sometimes people fear that they are physically unattractive to their partners. Other times, they may not feel respected for their careers or accomplishments. These insecurities may lead to jealousy in the relationship and a desire to control whom your partner interacts with for fear that they may find other people more attractive. In turn, the partner may push you away, rebel and act out, or lie about their social interactions to avoid a jealous response. These behaviors may lead to more betrayal that ultimately could result in an affair.

Let's again take a look at the couples from Chapter 2 to examine some of the factors that may have led to their affairs. I've included the original stories again and highlighted in bold print the areas that give us a contextual understanding of why these affairs occurred.

Story #1: Marjorie and Devon

Marjorie is married and has two young children with her husband, Devon, who is their primary caretaker throughout the day. Marjorie has been successful at her job, which requires her to travel frequently. She feels the responsibility of financially taking care of the family, **but also feels stressed when she is at home** *because of the kids and her difficult relationship with Devon. Devon feels overwhelmed by the demands of caring for the children and gets frustrated when Marjorie has to travel, which often* **leads to arguments. The more they argue, the more time Marjorie spends away from the house. She feels criticized and unappreciated.** *During this time, a male coworker named Dan starts to* **show her more and more attention.** *He is single with no children and seems to* **appreciate Marjorie's dedication to work, as well as her intelligence.**

At first Marjorie and Dan only spend time together at the office for work, and then occasionally go to lunch to discuss a business project. Marjorie starts to feel a bit guilty, but is able to **justify their meetings as necessary for her job.** *Months go by, and Dan gets a promotion and starts to travel to the same conferences that Marjorie attends. As their friendship grows, it* **gradually becomes flirtatious.** *Marjorie* **enjoys the attention and tells herself that there is nothing wrong with flirting back a little.** *This behavior goes on for a while until they are together at a conference out of town and* **meet for a drink at**

Step 3: Understanding Why the Affair Occurred

the end of the day. *That night, they end up having sex. Marjorie feels guilty, but is able to **justify the relationship in her mind**. She **tells herself that Devon has no time for her, has not been interested in sex for months, and only finds ways to criticize her**. Marjorie also convinces herself that **if Devon doesn't know about the other guy, it won't hurt him**. After all, **she deserves to be happy, and it is not really hurting anyone if he doesn't know**.*

<u>Devon's Emotional Response to the Affair</u>

When Devon finds out about the affair Marjorie was having with her coworker, he feels shocked, angry, hurt, disappointed, insecure, sad, embarrassed, and disgusted. He is shocked by the fact that Marjorie did this after he never, ever thought she could. She has always been an ethical person and speaks negatively about people who cheat on their spouses. He is angry that she chose to do this to him and the family in light of all of the possible consequences of her behaviors. He feels devastatingly hurt. Since he has a hard time opening up to other people, he has relied on Marjorie as his sole confidante, yet now she has betrayed his trust completely. He is disappointed that Marjorie has chosen to behave this way. Again, the affair seems totally out of character for her and the way she was raised. Devon feels insecure. He is a stay-at-home dad, and if this event ends their relationship, will he and the kids be okay? He is sad for himself and the kids. Will this mean the end of his relationship with Marjorie and the end of their family being all together? He is also embarrassed about the situation because everyone in their community seems to admire their relationship, and if other people found out about the infidelity, they may think differently about them and their family. Devon also feels disgusted when images of Marjorie and this other guy being intimate together come up in his mind. Eventually, he is able to communicate these and other emotions to Marjorie.

Why Did Marjorie Have this Affair?

As you can see from the highlighted areas above, Marjorie was unhappy in her primary relationship with Devon. They argued a lot, she felt stressed at home, and she felt unappreciated and criticized by Devon. She did what a lot of people do in these unhappy situations: she simply avoided it. Instead of addressing her feelings of discontent in a healthy way with Devon, she worked longer hours, and generally avoided going home. She tried to talk with Devon about her feelings, but wasn't direct enough with him. She believed that the friction between them might get better on its own, and didn't realize how far apart they were becoming because of how gradually it was happening. Marjorie didn't consider couples therapy because she blamed Devon for most of their problems.

The other factor that contributed to Marjorie's affair was her justifying thought process. She made up reasons why her behaviors weren't so bad and why it would be best for Devon not to disclose them to him. She also wanted to avoid dealing with the fallout from this affair and didn't want to have to leave this new exciting relationship.

Story #2: Sherry and Abraham

Sherry always wanted to get married and have children. She has been married to Abraham for ten years and has willingly given up her career to take care of their son. However, Sherry has been **increasingly dissatisfied with her life. She doesn't feel successful as a mother** *due to her son's challenging behavior.* **She also doesn't feel attractive to her husband,** *who has become more distant over the years. Sherry* **misses the time when she was appreciated at work and pursued by Abraham.**

Step 3: Understanding Why the Affair Occurred

*Recently, her son's soccer coach Manuel has been spending more time speaking with her at practices. In fact, he gave Sherry his cell phone number to call in case she had any questions about how her son is doing in soccer. This quickly turns into daily phone conversations about her unhappiness in life. Manuel is such a good listener and seems to genuinely understand and care about her. One day, when they are talking on the phone, he suggests meeting for coffee to continue their conversation face to face. Since her son is at school, they start to meet frequently during the day. Sherry finds herself looking forward to their meetings more than anything in her life. Soon, Manuel begins to tell her how wonderful and beautiful she is and soon after, they begin a physical relationship. Sherry feels terrible about their relationship, but **feels obsessed with getting together with him**. **She loves the way he pursues her and values her intelligence, humor, and beauty**.*

Abraham's Emotional Response to the Affair

When Abraham finds out about Sherry's affair, he feels angry, hurt, disappointed, disrespected, disgusted, frustrated, hopeless and unappreciated. He feels angry that his wife was spending so much time with another man and was physical with him. He feels hurt that she would do something like this to him after he has always been faithful to her. He feels disappointed that Sherry would engage in these behaviors and wonders if he ever really knew the real Sherry. He feels disrespected by Sherry's engaging in behaviors with another man while he was working hard to support the family. He feels disgusted when he thinks about Sherry and the other guy spending time together and being physically intimate with each other. He feels frustrated that she didn't talk with him first and initiate couples counseling before she chose to get involved with this guy. Abraham feels hopeless that he may never be able to forgive her, and their relationship might be tarnished forever. He feels unappreciated for working so hard to create a stable, financially secure life for Sherry and the family while she was spending her time and energy thinking about and developing a relationship with another man. Abraham also has many other emotions about this affair and eventually is able to communicate them to Sherry both in and out of therapy.

<u>Why Did Sherry Have this Affair?</u>

Sherry has always been a high achiever and derived her self-esteem and self-worth from her accomplishments. She believed the best thing for her kids was to give up her career and be a full-time mom, but quickly felt dissatisfied with this role. To deal with her guilt for feeling this way, she has tried to bury her feelings and just move forward. She also has been bored with life and therefore very receptive to things that feel more exciting, such as a new relationship. Before she realized it, Sherry was almost addicted to the exhilarating feelings of being in this new relationship, and it was difficult to let go of it. Part of her has felt guilty about how this affair might be hurting Abraham, but the stronger part of her has felt excited and alive. In short, she felt better about herself and her life when she was in this new relationship.

Story #3: Steve and Jessica

Steve was **exposed to sex at an early age when an older child in the neighborhood used to show him pornography when he was just eight years old**. By the time Steve was 13, he was looking online at pornographic videos and started to masturbate on a regular basis. Through high school and college, Steve would masturbate more often, **especially when he was experiencing stress in his life**. At 30, Steve

Step 3: Understanding Why the Affair Occurred

is currently in a committed relationship that he hopes will eventually turn into marriage. He has hidden his daily porn behaviors from his girlfriend Jessica, and hopes that being in a relationship will help him stop fantasizing so much about other women. However, he finds himself continually looking at pornography and eventually starts to reach out to escort services. He loves Jessica and hopes that she never finds out. One day, he hopes to be completely faithful to her and end his other sexual behaviors, but for now **he feels trapped by his need for the comfort and stress relief these behaviors provide him.** *Steve is miserable.* **He doesn't know why he can't stop doing what he is doing.**

<u>Jessica's Emotional Response to the Affair</u>

When Jessica finds out about Steve's betraying behaviors, she feels shocked, hurt, guarded, confused, disgusted, abandoned, unattractive and hopeless. She feels shocked because of the length of time and frequency of these behaviors. She feels hurt that Steve didn't disclose some of his behaviors earlier in their relationship so she would know what she was getting into and they might have been able to address them together. She feels guarded now because she feels she can't trust anything about Steve and needs to be careful not to get hurt anymore. She feels confused about why Steve would engage in such behaviors when they had such an active and seemingly enjoyable physical relationship. She feels disgusted when imagining Steve with other women. She feels abandoned by him after he formerly actively pursued her and told her he wanted to marry her. She feels unattractive when she compares herself to escorts and women in pornography. She feels hopeless, wondering whether Steve will ever be able to stop engaging in these behaviors. If he can't, will they ever make it together? Along with these emotions, Jessica talks with Steve about many others she experienced after finding out about Steve's behaviors over the years.

Why Did Steve Have this Affair?

Steve was exposed to sex and sexual feelings before he was able to understand and process these feelings in a healthy way. He started to use pornography and masturbation as a coping mechanism early on in his life and continued these behaviors into adulthood. Steve essentially became addicted to these behaviors and then escalated them by hiring escorts. He felt ashamed of his sexual activities, but the more shame he felt, the more stress he felt, and the more he would engage in these behaviors to relieve the stress. Sex was an escape from life's worries and the shame he felt on a regular basis.

Steve never wanted to share any of this with Jessica because he worried she would be disgusted by him and maybe even leave him if she knew about them. He also believed that he could stop these behaviors by himself so that he'd never have to deal with their fallout in his relationship with Jessica.

Of course, these are not the only reasons people have affairs. The reasons are complex and multiple, and take time to sort through and understand. Often they can even be traced to childhood traumas or pain. The better you understand why you ended up in an affair, the more effectively you will be to keep it from happening again.

For example, if alcohol or drugs were significant factors, you may need to cut back, stop using these substances altogether, or set up some significant boundaries around their use. If unhappiness and dysfunction in your primary relationship was a major factor, you should seek couples counseling not only to repair the relationship after the affair, but also to help resolve ongoing issues and strengthen the relationship. You may need to address insecurities in individual therapy to heal past hurts and increase self-esteem.

Step 3: Understanding Why the Affair Occurred

In order to lower the likelihood that an affair will happen again, these issues must be addressed. The best predictor of future behavior is past behavior—unless the behaviors leading up to the affair have been properly addressed. If you want your partner to forgive you and trust you again, they are going to need to see significant changes in you and a willingness to seek help when needed.

Step 3 is about understanding the factors that led up to the affair so that you as a couple can identify and address individual and relationship issues that existed beforehand. This step is not about making excuses, but rather about becoming self-aware. The ultimate goal of this self-awareness is forgiving yourself, whether or not your partner can forgive you.

The Shame Effect

Shame can be the number-one enemy that keeps you from being honest and forthcoming about what happened. We have already discussed the use of shame shields to avoid dealing with your shame. Another way a person who has had an affair can try to avoid the pain of shame is to overreact to their own behaviors and oversimplify the truth. By saying that you are a hopeless cause or that you don't deserve a second chance, you are choosing not to explore the factors and reasons leading up to the affair. Blanket statements about your own unworthiness can keep you from reaching the truth and can also keep your partner from getting to their own point of forgiveness.

Instead of overreacting or oversimplifying, I recommend spending some time alone actually feeling the discomfort of shame, and getting to know the causes of it. Keeping a journal or talking to a supportive friend or therapist can help you discover where the shame is coming from so that eventually you and your partner may be ready for the last step: asking for and receiving forgiveness.

Truths and Tips to Hold On To

❖ Affairs usually happen over time and involve a series of decisions and factors leading up to them.

❖ Before you begin to explore the factors that contributed to an affair, make sure you and your partner have developed enough empathy during Step 2. Otherwise, the reasons for the affair will sound more like excuses.

❖ Unhappiness in a relationship, whether because of conflict or disconnection, can make a partner susceptible to outside influences and temptations that might lead to an affair.

❖ Examining what your relationship was like before the affair began may give you and your partner a better understanding of why it happened and also guide you in the future to healthier dynamics.

❖ Often a partner's unhappiness about aspects of their life that have nothing to do with their relationship can contribute to an affair.

❖ Clinical depression, poor physical health, financial troubles, problems at work, and feelings around aging are all factors that can contribute to unhappiness.

Step 3: Understanding Why the Affair Occurred

- ❖ Using alcohol or drugs to tune out can cause many behaviors that contribute to an affair such as emotional disconnection between partners, poor judgment, a tug-of-war to manage the alcohol or drug consumption, or behavior that offends or hurts your partner.

- ❖ For the betrayer, you may try to avoid shame by oversimplifying and overreacting to your affair behaviors instead of dealing with the real factors that led to the affair.

- ❖ Keeping a journal or talking to a friend or therapist will help you practice being vulnerable so that you do not resort to these avoidance behaviors.

Now that you as a couple have an understanding about the different factors that led to the affair, you can move on to the next chapter, which describes the ultimate goal of my 4-Step Affair Recovery Process: forgiveness.

CHAPTER 10

Step 4: The Leap of Faith

Once you have thoroughly worked through Steps 1–3, you are ready for Step 4. Hopefully, the chasm between you as a couple has narrowed and healing has begun. However, there will still be some hesitancy for the betrayed individual to put their trust back into their partner due to the risks of getting hurt again. Ultimately, this step will require a leap of faith, because nothing is guaranteed. No one can predict the future, and the reality is that an affair could happen again.

If you are both ready for this leap, I recommend the following: Each of you needs to write the other a letter. In these letters, you will summarize your experience of steps 1–3. In addition, the betrayer will recommit to the relationship and promise to do everything they can to minimize the likelihood of another affair. They then ask directly for their partner to forgive them and put faith back in them and the relationship. The person who was betrayed will, in addition to summarizing steps 1–3, promise to forgive their partner and put their faith back in them. They will agree to move beyond this traumatic situation. This will include their commitment to use the affair neither as a weapon nor as a justification for their own behavior moving forward, even in a fight. After these letters are written, they should be read aloud. This can happen either alone together or in the office of a therapist who can be a witness to the new commitments.

Here are examples of letters from the couples from Chapter 2.

Story #1: Marjorie and Devon

Marjorie's Letter

Dear Devon,

I know that I betrayed you when I stayed away from home more and more, and developed a relationship with a coworker to the point that it became sexual. I also betrayed you by keeping this all a secret and by lying to you about it. (Step 1) I know that as a result of these behaviors, you felt disappointed, hurt, and disgusted. I know that it also made you feel insecure about yourself and about our future together. More than you know, I regret causing you so much pain. (Step 2) I realize now that I was just running from our problems instead of facing them with you or with the help of a therapist. I also realize that I should have been more direct with you about how I was feeling, so you could have had an opportunity to respond to my needs. I shouldn't ever have blamed you for the problems we were having, but instead, I should have taken responsibility by doing something about them. (Step 3) I am 100% committed to addressing these issues by continuing to seek counseling until we both feel better about our relationship. I am also committed to regularly communicating with you about how I'm feeling and to being open to hearing how you are feeling. I'm asking you today to forgive me for cheating on you. I am promising you that I will do everything in my power never to let this happen again. I love you and I am fully committed to you.

Love,

Marjorie

Step 4: The Leap of Faith

<u>Devon's Letter</u>

Dear Marjorie,

When you were staying away from home and then I discovered that you were sleeping with a coworker and lying to me about your entire relationship with him (Step 1), I was shocked. I never imagined that you would do something like this and I was hurt, sad, and disappointed. I wondered if we could ever recover from this and was anxious about our future together and the future of our family. (Step 2) I know that you were really unhappy in our relationship and that you chose to run away from these problems rather than face them. I also realize you had a difficult time expressing your feelings to me and started to avoid coming home or spending time with me. (Step 3) Over the past few months, you have demonstrated that you love me and are committed to our relationship by your patience and commitment to this process of forgiveness. Even though I know that nothing in the future is certain, I am choosing today to forgive you and move forward in our relationship. I promise not to use this affair as a weapon or to ever use it as a justification for my own behavior in the future. I love you and I am committed to you.

Love,

Devon

Story #2: Sherry and Abraham

Sherry's Letter

Dear Abraham,

I know when I started to talk with our son's coach privately, met with him, and then had a sexual relationship with him, I betrayed my vows to you. I realize now that even talking with him about personal things without letting you know was not okay. (Step 1) Because of what I did, you felt hurt, angry, disrespected, and unappreciated. I also realize that you have felt anxiety about our future and have had difficulty trusting me every time I leave the house. I know this whole thing has been extremely difficult for you to deal with and has also made it more difficult for you to focus on your work. (Step 2) I accept that part of the reason I made these unhealthy choices is that I was unhappy with my life and maybe even a bit bored with being a full-time stay-at-home mother. I wish I had talked with you and a counselor about this sooner, before I ended up having this affair. I also realize that I have always put too much of my self-esteem and self-worth into what I accomplish in life, and I commit to working on this in counseling. (Step 3) I accept full responsibility for my actions and promise to do everything in my power never to let this happen again. I also promise to be open and honest with you about how I am feeling and what I need in our relationship. I love you and I am committed to our relationship.

Love,

Sherry

Step 4: The Leap of Faith

<u>Abraham's Letter</u>

Dear Sherry,

I love you very much. When I found out that you had cheated on me with our son's coach (Step 1), I was so angry and hurt. I felt disrespected, sad, and hopeless at times. I wondered if we would ever recover from this. (Step 2) Through counseling, I have realized that part of the reason you had this affair is that you have been unhappy for quite some time. I know that part of your unhappiness was caused by my tendency to pull away from you and focus too much on work. I didn't realize until recently how much this affected you. (Step 3) I want you to know that I forgive you. I trust you when you say you love me and are committed to me, and I am also committed to you. Moving forward, I promise to be more available in our relationship. I also promise not to ever use this affair as a weapon or an excuse for anything I do that may hurt you in the future.

Love,

Abraham

Story #3: Steve and Jessica

Steve's Letter

Dear Jessica,

I realize that when I kept my past from you and started to engage in sexual activities such as looking at pornography and contacting escort services, I betrayed your trust in me. (Step 1) You have every reason to feel betrayed and hopeless about the possibility of ever trusting me again. In addition, after finding out about what I did, I know you felt insecure about your attractiveness and worried about whether I would ever fully be satisfied with you as my partner. I know that you want and expect me to turn only to you for sexual connection. I want that too. (Step 2) Through counseling, I have learned that I struggle with a sex addiction that needs to be addressed and treated in order for me to stop acting out in this way. I know that I have used sex as a coping mechanism and want to learn how to find healthier ways to cope with stress in my life. (Step 3) I am fully committed to continuing my individual counseling and couples counseling until you, my counselors, and I feel that counseling is no longer necessary. Please forgive me and put your trust back in me. I love you.

Love,

Steve

Step 4: The Leap of Faith

Jessica's Letter

Dear Steve,

When I found out that you had lied to me about your past and kept it secret from me, I didn't know what to do or think. Then when I found out that you regularly looked at pornography and had gone even as far as contacting escort services (Step 1), I felt overwhelmed and hopeless. I felt insecure about my attractiveness to you as well as about your commitment to me. I felt concerned about our future together and worried that we might never be able to get married and have the life and relationship that we had dreamed about together. (Step 2) Even though all of this affected me deeply, finding out that you struggle with sex addiction issues helped me understand you more. I understand now that you have childhood wounds that contributed to these impulses and see that you have been dedicated to therapy and healing. (Step 3) Even given the risk, I am choosing today to forgive you for these behaviors and put my faith in you. I commit to our relationship and to not using these issues and past behaviors as weapons against you. I also commit to never using these behaviors as any excuse for my future actions in our relationship.

Love,

Jessica

As you can see from the preceding examples, the letters are unique but also follow a prescribed pattern to help guide couples in expressing their experiences in a healthy and productive way. This pattern structures the letters and includes the important part of Step 4, the Leap of Faith. I recommend that, in addition to writing and reading these letters to each other, couples agree on a meaningful gesture or ceremony that represents their new beginning and re-commitment in their relationship. This can be something as simple as exchanging special gifts or as complex as planning and participating in a ceremony to renew their vows in front of their family and friends. The important part of this activity is to signify a milestone: when the relationship moves from broken to healed, and when you as a couple begin a new, healthier stage in your lives together.

Forgiving your partner does not mean saying their actions were not a big deal. In fact, what they did had a significant impact on you. Forgiving your partner does not "let them off the hook" and imply their behaviors were okay. Forgiveness is not a guarantee that these behaviors will never happen again. No one can guarantee what will happen in the future. Instead, forgiveness is choosing to trust your partner even though there are no guarantees.

Moving forward, both of you need to keep an eye out for signs of distress in the relationship and address these issues directly, either together or with a trusted therapist. Signs to look for include feelings of boredom or dissatisfaction in yourself or your partner, distance between the two of you, or an increase in arguments without resolution. The more a relationship is nurtured and the earlier problems are addressed, the less likely there will be problems that could lead to another affair.

Forgiveness is not amnesia. Both parties will still have memories of the affair and how it affected them. Triggers that bring back emotions and memories will also come up. They may happen on anniversaries of the events, while you are watching movies or television shows, or even in the presence of certain smells or music. Forgiveness means accepting that triggers will occur, but ensures that both of you will be open and loving towards each other when they happen. When you do feel these triggers of emotion, you need to talk about them with your partner and express empathy toward each other. Doing so can be a productive way to continue the healing and connection process, even though forgiveness has already occurred months (or even years) in the past. Painful memories can also bring appreciation for how far the relationship has developed, and the healing that has taken place.

The Shame Effect

As we know, according to Brené Brown, shame is "the intensely painful feeling or experience of believing we are flawed and therefore unworthy of acceptance and belonging." This belief can keep you from understanding that you are worthy of forgiveness and can hinder you from accepting your partner's leap of faith in this last step. Simply put, if shame is preventing you from feeling worthy of forgiveness, then you can't receive it. According to Brown, you can build resilience to shame by connecting with your own feelings. Hopefully by now, you have acquired some of the tools to do this. Resilience to shame involves moving toward empathy and away from fear, blame, and disconnection from yourself and from your partner.

Some of these tools include understanding why you are feeling shame, speaking openly about it with your partner or therapist, and reaching out to a supportive friend. In addition, recognizing your shame shields will help you know when shame is present. These shame shields include moving against your partner by being aggressive, moving away from your partner by withdrawing, or moving toward your partner by people-pleasing. Staying aware of these shields is crucial to building your shame resilience so that you can succeed in this last step.

Step 4: The Leap of Faith

Truths and Tips to Hold On To

- ❖ The last step asking for and offering forgiveness is called The Leap of Faith because there are no guarantees that betrayal won't happen again.

- ❖ Writing letters to each other that summarize the first three steps and promising to do everything possible to make sure betrayal won't happen again will help you make this leap of faith as a couple.

- ❖ A special act or ceremony after you have read these letters out loud to each other will signify the milestone when you as a couple move to a new, healthier stage in your lives together.

- ❖ Forgiveness does not minimize your partner's betrayal behaviors, nor does it guarantee that they will never happen again.

- ❖ Forgiveness means choosing to trust your partner again, even without this guarantee.

- ❖ Moving forward, you and your partner must continue to look for signs of distress in your relationship, including boredom, dissatisfaction, disconnection, and unresolved arguments.

- ❖ Forgiveness also means accepting that triggers will occur that remind you of the betrayal behaviors.

- ❖ Discussing these triggers openly with your partner and expressing empathy toward each other will continue the healing process, even long after the initial forgiveness has occurred.

- ❖ Painful memories can act as a positive marker of how far your relationship has come since the initial betrayal took place.

- ❖ As the betrayer, shame can make you feel unworthy of receiving your partner's forgiveness in this last step.

- ❖ By continuing to be vulnerable with those you trust, you can build up a resilience to shame that ultimately will help you accept your partner's forgiveness.

CHAPTER 11

Factors that Affect Recovery

Because each couple and each situation is different, my process will not work the same way for everyone. As a couples counselor, I have identified factors that affect how successful the 4-Step Affair Recovery Process will be and how long it will take. Here they are, listed in general descending order of importance:

Factor #1: The Level of Commitment/Motivation of the Betrayer

The level of commitment and motivation to heal the relationship on the part of the person who had the affair is crucial. This journey will be difficult for both individuals; however, the betrayer will have to show their willingness to pursue their partner and ask for forgiveness. As I mentioned earlier, this preliminary period involves a number of steps that can be extremely challenging. First, you must be willing to end the affair relationship completely. Even if you don't feel any emotional connection with this person, you may need to change jobs if the affair happened with a coworker, or change churches or neighborhoods if these are places the affair began. This step may mean seriously hurting the other person in the affair. It may also involve your experiencing symptoms similar to withdrawal from alcohol or drugs if you were using the affair to escape your own unhappiness. Second, for my forgiveness process to work, you must continually be willing to put yourself in uncomfortable situations, such as asking regularly how your partner is feeling about the affair and being open to hearing this information. Third, you might find it difficult to be as transparent as possible about your schedule, your whereabouts, and the company you keep as you and your partner rebuild trust. Finally, you will need to have a tremendous amount of patience and courage to be available day after day and month after month for your partner while the healing process takes place.

Factor #2: The Level of Commitment/Motivation of the Betrayed

The commitment and motivation of the person who was betrayed are also very important. Although you are not the one who had the affair, you have to be willing to participate in the forgiveness process, even though it can feel very painful, stressful, and risky. You will need to listen to what happened, talk about how it emotionally affected you, and explore why your partner had the affair. All of these steps require extreme vulnerability and can disrupt parts of your daily life, including eating and sleeping routines, parenting, and work. Ultimately, my forgiveness process takes a lot of courage, especially when it is time to take the leap of faith and put your trust back in your partner. You will need to make yourself vulnerable for this last step, but it is one that is necessary for finalizing the act of forgiveness.

Factor #3: The Strength/Weakness of the Relationship before the Betrayal Occurred

Almost all relationships that experience affairs had some problems before the affair occurred. However, some relationships are stronger or weaker than others. The more significant the problems in your relationship and the longer these problems have existed, the more difficult it will be to move through the forgiveness process. For example, if you as a couple have always had difficulty discussing your emotions in healthy ways, it will be more difficult to do so during the forgiveness process. If you have been distant for a while, you or your partner may be less motivated to repair the relationship. If you have a history of explosive conversations, you will need to practice extra patience to really listen to your partner and not lash out with hurtful words when anger arises.

Factor #4: The Level of Attachment of the Betrayer to the Other Person

As I said earlier, to repair your relationship, you must cut all ties with the person you had the affair with. If you are emotionally attached to this person, it will be a difficult and painful process. Attachment can occur whether or not a physical relationship took place. In fact, some physical relationships have very little emotional attachment present. When attachment exists, even if contact with this person is cut off, you may still think about them and, consequently, feel that the other person is still in between you and your primary partner. This experience can distract you from the emotional work you need to do to repair your relationship and can hinder your progress as a couple.

Factor #5: The Duration of the Affair/Betrayal

A short instance of cheating may be extremely painful and damaging to a relationship. The longer the infidelity lasts, the more damaging it can be because the level of emotional attachment involved makes it more difficult to end the relationship. A longer affair can also be more damaging because the lying and deceit took place for longer periods of time, making it that much more difficult to repair the trust that was broken.

Factor #6: The Level of Emotional Intelligence, Empathy, and Communication Skills

The greater a person's ability to understand their own and others' emotions, the better equipped they are to participate in the forgiveness process. This is true whether you are the one who had the affair or the partner who is trying to forgive. The empathy step is one of the most important steps in my forgiveness process, yet everyone has different levels of skill to understand other people's emotions and to communicate that understanding. If you or your partner have difficulty with these skills, it would be wise and beneficial to work with an individual therapist while you are working to repair your relationship.

Truths and Tips to Hold On To

- ❖ The most important factor when a couple is trying to heal from an affair is the betrayer's level of commitment to the process. It is up to you to lead the way in restoring the trust that has been broken.

- ❖ A willingness to cut off all ties with the other person is crucial to healing from the affair.

- ❖ You can show your commitment to healing your relationship by checking in with your partner regularly, being completely transparent about your schedule, and being very patient.

- ❖ As the betrayed, you will need to be committed to the process as well. Extreme amounts of courage and vulnerability will be needed for you to listen to what happened and stay open about your feelings.

- ❖ The health of your primary relationship before the betrayal plays a significant role in your ability to heal as a couple.

- ❖ The length of the affair can affect the ability for you to heal, depending on how attached you have become to the other person and also how long you have been deceiving your partner.

- ❖ Emotional intelligence, empathy, and communications skills all play important roles in how well a couple will heal from an affair.

CHAPTER 12

A Message of Hope

Affairs can be devastating. They turn worlds upside down and have ripple effects that hurt many people. Most people don't believe they will ever have an affair or be in a relationship with someone who cheats on them. Many also believe they would definitely choose to leave a relationship if their partner had an affair. However, affairs and responses to them are complicated and can challenge our pre-existing beliefs about our responses and ourselves. Often, choosing to leave a relationship involves saying goodbye to a partner you have grown emotionally attached to, perhaps for a long period of time. Your decision to leave will also affect your children. Additionally, ending a relationship often affects extended family and friends, and may disrupt your place in the community.

I am not suggesting that all relationships can recover from an affair, but I recommend that most people at least consider the possibility of healing and reconciliation. Even if the relationship eventually ends, working through this forgiveness process will help future relationships. In addition, if a couple who is raising children breaks up, healing will help them be the best co-parents possible with the understanding that, following separation or divorce, they will still be part of each other's lives.

You might be surprised to know that many lives are positively affected through this process. I have witnessed this time and time again in my practice. Couples who feel devastated and hopeless have been able to recover and reconcile through hard work, courage, patience, and persistence. In fact, many of these couples end up commenting that the affair was the most difficult experience they have ever endured, but one that ended up propelling them to a deeper and more satisfying relationship than they ever could have imagined. My hope for you is that you give this process a chance to help you discover whether your relationship can evolve to this place of love and connection. Not only will you be giving yourselves a gift as a couple and as individuals, but, if you have children together, you might also be bringing a blessing to your children and the other important people in your lives.

Brené Brown says the following:

> *Forgiveness is not forgetting or walking away from accountability or condoning a hurtful act. It is the process of taking back and healing our lives so we can truly live.*

My greatest wish in writing this book is that you as a couple have been able to experience the healing that only forgiveness can bring after an affair. I hope that my 4-Step Affair Recovery Process will inspire you on the rest of your journey, whether as a couple or as individuals, to continue to grow.

APPENDIX

Truths and Tips to Hold On To

Chapter 1: Questions, Questions, Questions

- ❖ Questions are a normal part of the healing process after an affair.

- ❖ It is important to address these questions directly, even if the answers are not immediately forthcoming.

- ❖ Until these questions are addressed, you will not have the clarity you need to make decisions about moving forward in your relationship.

- ❖ Because people outside of your relationship will have varying opinions, be careful about whom you choose to speak to about the affair.

- ❖ You should never blame yourself (or take the blame for) your partner's infidelity.

- ❖ Cognitive dissonance, the state of having inconsistent thoughts or beliefs, is a normal response to an affair.

- ❖ Assimilation, the reconciliation of seemingly opposing truths, is an important step in the healing process after an affair.

Chapter 2: Anatomy of an Affair

- ❖ An affair can take many different forms, including flirtatious behavior, a secret emotional connection, a sexual encounter, or looking at pornography.

- ❖ Each couple has implicit and explicit agreements about what constitutes betrayal.

- ❖ Some signs of problem behavior in a relationship include keeping secrets from your partner, outright lying, or omitting information.

- ❖ Our culture teaches that true passion in a relationship lasts forever, a misconception that can lead to feelings of disappointment that cause us to look outside of our relationship for happiness.

- ❖ Feelings of guilt and shame are indicators that your behavior could be perceived as a form of betrayal by your partner.

- ❖ As in the metaphor of the boiling frog, an affair can often creep up gradually, drawing a person in without their full awareness.

- ❖ Alcohol often plays a significant role in poor judgment that leads to an affair.

Chapter 3: Managing the Initial Crisis as a Couple

- ❖ Setting aside a certain limited time each day to discuss the affair will give structure to the conversation and also ensure that feelings and questions will get addressed.

- ❖ Be careful to keep your children protected from overhearing conversations about the affair.

- ❖ Take the word *divorce* and other exit statements out of your vocabulary for at least three months.

- ❖ Do not make any major decisions about your relationship, living situation, or job until you are out of this crisis phase.

- ❖ Do not talk about the affair late at night or if one or both of you have been drinking.

- ❖ Choose only one or two people in your inner circle to talk to about the affair. These people should be trustworthy and able to manage their own emotions about the situation.

- ❖ Prioritize self-care at this time to make sure that you are both at your personal best to deal with the intensity of what's happening.

Chapter 4: Managing the Initial Crisis as Individuals

❖ As the betrayed, consider carefully which questions you really want answers to.

❖ As the betrayed, pull back from investigating further details about the affair if you find your thoughts keeping you awake or if you can't concentrate on life responsibilities.

❖ As the betrayed, acts of revenge may feel good in the short term. However, they may create difficulties for you in the future if you decide to move forward in your relationship.

❖ As the betrayer, telling the truth is of utmost importance if you wish to rebuild trust in your relationship.

❖ As the betrayer, remaining calm and listening are key indicators to your partner that you understand the pain your actions have caused and that you are committed to working things out.

❖ As the betrayer, do not offer your partner any explanations for your behavior at this early stage, since they will only sound like excuses.

❖ As the betrayer, seeing your own individual therapist to explore the reasons for your affair may not only help you find clarity, but also help your partner to be more patient about hearing explanations.

Chapter 5: Forgiveness

- ❖ Forgiveness is not a favor you do for your partner, saying that they owe you something in return.
- ❖ Forgiveness often takes time.
- ❖ Forgiveness is not forgetting that a betrayal has taken place.
- ❖ Forgiveness is not a guarantee that you won't feel pain, anger, shame, or guilt anymore.
- ❖ Forgiveness involves promising your partner that you will not punish them for their betrayal.
- ❖ Forgiveness is deciding not to use your partner's affair as an excuse for your own poor behaviors.

Chapter 6: Steps in the Forgiveness Process

❖ Before you can begin the 4-Step Affair Recovery Process, reestablishing trust as a couple is key.

❖ Ways to reestablish trust include sharing passwords to computers and phones, sharing details about your whereabouts and the people you are with, spending more time at home, and suspending business trips.

❖ The trust-building agreements you establish with your partner should last at least 6–12 months before you discuss changing them.

❖ Step One in the forgiveness process involves sharing as much information as you can about the facts of the affair.

❖ Step Two is about developing empathy by communicating feelings honestly and constructively.

❖ Step Three establishes contextual understanding about the betrayal and answers the question "Why did this happen?"

❖ Step Four is called The Leap of Faith and requires the betrayer to ask for forgiveness and the betrayed to commit to forgiving.

Truths and Tips to Hold On To

Chapter 7: Step 1: What Actually Happened?

❖ The betrayer needs to be as transparent as possible about the facts involved in the affair, even if they worry about hurting their partner further.

❖ The betrayed has the right to ask any questions about what happened but should wait to ask questions about their partner's around the affair until dealing with the context of the affair in Step Three.

❖ Both partners should discuss what parts of the affair were actual betrayals of their contract—which, in general, is any behavior or information the betrayer intentionally kept from their partner.

❖ Once you have completed the 4-Step Affair Recovery Process, you and your partner should get clear on what the boundaries of your relationship need to be from now on.

❖ For the betrayer, shame about your behaviors can often make you feel unlovable, making you reluctant to tell the entire truth.

❖ Building shame resilience by choosing to continue to be vulnerable ultimately will help you and your partner heal.

Chapter 8: Step 2: Empathy for the Betrayed

- ❖ For the betrayer, true empathy involves listening to your partner's feelings and being able to reflect them clearly and thoughtfully.

- ❖ For the betrayed, describing your emotions to your partner in as much detail as possible will help you feel better understood so that you can eventually heal from your pain.

- ❖ Common emotions that come up for the betrayed partner include shock, anger, disappointment, anxiety, sadness, and grief. These are all normal.

- ❖ For the betrayer, developing increasing empathy is important before moving on to the next step in the forgiveness process when you will discuss the reasons why the affair happened. Otherwise, if your partner doesn't feel understood, they are likely to perceive these reasons as excuses for your behaviors.

- ❖ For the betrayer, showing empathy may include actively nodding when listening to your partner, being willing to share passwords to devices, saying phrases like "I'm so sorry," and being patient with your partner when they repeatedly ask questions.

- ❖ Conversely, certain behaviors such as getting frustrated, rolling your eyes, sighing, sharing too much about your own feelings, and pursuing your partner physically or sexually can show a lack of empathy.

- ❖ As the betrayer, the shame you feel about your affair may cause you to develop shame shields, which are strategies of disconnection and self-protection.

- ❖ Recognizing these shame shields that can move you against, away from, or toward your partner in unhealthy ways will help you to stay honest and vulnerable in your conversations.

Chapter 9: Step 3: Understanding Why the Affair Occurred

- ❖ Affairs usually happen over time and involve a series of decisions and factors leading up to them.
- ❖ Before you begin to explore the factors that contributed to an affair, make sure you and your partner have developed enough empathy during Step 2. Otherwise, the reasons for the affair will sound more like excuses.
- ❖ Unhappiness in a relationship, whether because of conflict or disconnection, can make a partner susceptible to outside influences and temptations that might lead to an affair.
- ❖ Examining what your relationship was like before the affair began may give you and your partner a better understanding of why it happened and also guide you in the future to healthier dynamics.
- ❖ Often a partner's unhappiness about aspects of their life that have nothing to do with their relationship can contribute to an affair.
- ❖ Clinical depression, poor physical health, financial troubles, problems at work, and feelings around aging are all factors that can contribute to unhappiness.
- ❖ Using alcohol or drugs to tune out can cause many behaviors that contribute to an affair such as emotional disconnection between partners, poor judgment, a tug-of-war to manage the alcohol or drug consumption, or behavior that offends or hurts your partner.
- ❖ For the betrayer, you may try to avoid shame by oversimplifying and overreacting to your affair behaviors instead of dealing with the real factors that led to the affair.
- ❖ Keeping a journal or talking to a friend or therapist will help you practice being vulnerable so that you do not resort to these avoidance behaviors.

Chapter 10: Step 4: The Leap of Faith

- ❖ The last step asking for and offering forgiveness is called The Leap of Faith because there are no guarantees that betrayal won't happen again.

- ❖ Writing letters to each other that summarize the first three steps and promising to do everything possible to make sure betrayal won't happen again will help you make this leap of faith as a couple.

- ❖ A special act or ceremony after you have read these letters out loud to each other will signify the milestone when you as a couple move to a new, healthier stage in your lives together.

- ❖ Forgiveness does not minimize your partner's betrayal behaviors, nor does it guarantee that they will never happen again.

- ❖ Forgiveness means choosing to trust your partner again, even without this guarantee.

- ❖ Moving forward, you and your partner must continue to look for signs of distress in your relationship, including boredom, dissatisfaction, disconnection, and unresolved arguments.

- ❖ Forgiveness also means accepting that triggers will occur that remind you of the betrayal behaviors.

Chapter 11: Factors that Affect Recovery

❖ The most important factor when a couple is trying to heal from an affair is the betrayer's level of commitment to the process. It is up to you to lead the way in restoring the trust that has been broken.

❖ A willingness to cut off all ties with the other person is crucial to healing from the affair.

❖ You can show your commitment to healing your relationship by checking in with your partner regularly, being completely transparent about your schedule, and being very patient.

❖ As the betrayed, you will need to be committed to the process as well. Extreme amounts of courage and vulnerability will be needed for you to listen to what happened and stay open about your feelings.

❖ The health of your primary relationship before the betrayal plays a significant role in your ability to heal as a couple.

❖ The length of the affair can affect the ability for you to heal, depending on how attached you have become to the other person and also how long you have been deceiving your partner.

❖ Emotional intelligence, empathy, and communications skills all play important roles in how well a couple will heal from an affair.

ABOUT THE AUTHOR
Andrew McConaghie, LCSW

Andrew McConaghie, LCSW and his wife, Tracy, opened McConaghie Counseling in Alpharetta, Georgia over twenty years ago. He has over thirty years of experience, specializing in couples counseling. In addition to working with clients, Andrew provides clinical consultation to couples therapists. As part of his clinical training, Andrew studied under John and Julie Gottman and Dr. Brené Brown. Andrew and his wife are also co-founders of the Upside Down Divorce® process that guides couples through a step-by-step approach to divorce that is healthy, good for children, and solution focused.

www.mcconaghiecounseling.com
www.upsidedowndivorce.com

Made in the USA
Columbia, SC
12 October 2021